OH NO HE DIDN'T!

Dating Advice
For
Men & Women
Based On
An Attorney's
15 Most
Outrageous
Dating Experiences.

ATTORNEY LISA D. WRIGHT

Published by
Attorney Wright, LLC

No names have been used and biographical data has been changed for the men detailed herein to protect their identities and their privacy.

This publication is intended to provide authoritative information regarding the subject matter covered. The publisher and author are not engaged in rendering legal or other professional services and do not have financial or commercial interests in any of the products or services mentioned in this book. If you require the services of an attorney or other expert assistance, you should seek the services of a competent attorney. The purchase of this book does not create an attorney-client relationship between the purchaser and Attorney Lisa D. Wright.

Oh No He Didn't! Dating Advice for Men & Women Based On An Attorney's 15 Most Outrageous Dating Experiences.

Published by Attorney Wright, LLC.

ISBN: 978-0-9845360-0-9

Printed in the United States of America.

ABOUT THE AUTHOR

Attorney Lisa D. Wright was born and raised in the Detroit, Michigan area. From 1986 – 1989 she attended Kentucky State University (KSU), pledged Delta Sigma Theta Sorority, Inc. and graduated with a Bachelor of Arts Degree in Accounting – Cum Laude with Business Departmental Honors at the age of 20. After KSU she worked as a Bank Examiner in Michigan before returning to graduate school.

From August 1996 – December 1999, she attended Duke University's School of Law and Fuqua School of Business to complete the Juris Doctorate (JD) and Masters of Business Administration (MBA) dual degree program in three and a half years.

In January 2000, she moved to Atlanta, Georgia to work in corporate America at as a marketing analyst and then as a corporate bankruptcy consultant.

In February 2001, she took the Georgia Bar examination for the first time and was notified in May 2001 that she passed. She then decided to actively pursue a legal career. In May 2002, she opened the Law Office of Lisa D.

Wright, LLC. Attorney Wright has represented clients with family law, criminal law, consumer law, and business law issues.

Oh No He Didn't! is Attorney Wright's first book. Attorney Lisa D. Wright is living in Atlanta, is single, is dating, and is looking forward to writing her next book.

Please visit her website at www.LisaDWright.com or email her at attorney@lisadwright.com. You may also follow Attorney Wright on Twitter at AttorneyWright.

AUTHOR'S ACKNOWLEDGMENTS

I would like to Acknowledge God and My Family for their love, support, vision, and encouragement throughout my outrageous life.

To my father, Marconi Wright, thank you for supporting my adventurous spirit, for encouraging my continued education, and for following me from up above. Aunt Oddie you're a great aunt, thanks for making the best sweet potato pies (www.auntoddies.com) over the years and for all of your support, my official Ohio publicist. To my sister Miki Wright thank you for your all of your love and support as I studied my way through two advanced degree programs, the CPA examination, and the bar examination. To my sister Nichon Wright thank you for all of my hair appointments, your hospitality during my visits to Detroit, and for repeatedly telling me to write this book...I am glad that I finally listened to you!

Thank you to Andrea Dennis for being a friend forever, for listening to my dating stories for over fifteen years, and for helping me edit and complete this book! Oh No He Didn't! would not have been possible without you.

To Crystal Cook (and the entire Cook Family), Kali Wilson-Beyah, and Lashawn Mikell, you are my extended family, my Delta Sigma Theta Sorority, Inc. Sorors, my informal Attorney advisors, and my Best Friends Forever!

To Larry Jemison (www.LarrySpeaks.com) thanks for calling to wish me a Happy 2010! Your call was a blessing in disguise. The advice and guidance that you shared with me for this project has been invaluable.

Soror Lois Mockabee thank you for helping me pick out my outfit for the cover of this book! A special thank you to Anita Norwood, you are a fabulous photographer, friend, and supporter!

Lastly, thank you to all of my friends and family that kept me motivated as I worked to complete this book: Rosalyn Bell, Jannie Eaddy, Julaine Golden, M. Fay Goodson, Vicki Lingley, LaShae Primus, Rico Richardson, Stephanie Sebree, Veronica Sentell, Filus Smith, and Michelle Walden. Your belief and support of me and this project made Oh No He Didn't! a reality.

CONTENTS

INTRODUCTION

I am sure that you have seen and heard the recent headlines about Chris Brown assaulting Rihanna after they had a heated argument; or Jon Gosselin declaring his extremely negative feelings towards his wife while their divorce was pending for their children and the rest of the world to hear; or South Carolina Governor Mark Sanford being dumb enough to tell his wife that he was going to try to fall back in love with her even though his Argentine mistress was his soul mate; or Tiger Woods leaving a voice mail message for his mistress asking her to do him a big favor and take her name off her voice mail greeting because his wife went through his cell phone and she may be giving her a call; or Jason Kidd having his fifth child with his second baby momma (and third mother of his children, as he also has 3 children with his ex-wife).

Every time I heard one of these stories I asked myself what were these men thinking? Somebody should have said something to them! Or, they should have called me and I literally would have told them what to do. Then as I reflected on my own dating experiences, I realized that I have dated men that acted just like Chris Brown, Jon Gosselin, Mark Sanford, Tiger Woods, and Jason Kidd! And when they needed some dating advice (whether they wanted it or not), I gave it to them! Oh No He Didn't! is a Dating Advice Guide based on my Outrageous Dating Experiences because these famous men are not the only ones that need some advice!

Oh No He Didn't! also provides advice for men that need assistance with mastering the fundamentals of dating. Have you ever been on a date and you didn't know what to say to a woman or how to keep the conversation going? Have you ever wanted to call a woman but you didn't know what you were going to say when she answered? Do you ever wonder what topics are off limits for text messaging? Have you ever created a Facebook page or an online dating profile and you weren't sure what information or photos to include? Well Oh No He Didn't! is going to provide you with the answers to all of these questions and more!

Oh No He Didn't! provides women with the advice they need to safely and confidently experience the joys of dating. Have you ever been on a date and wondered where in the world did he get his dating skills from and what you should do about it? Have you ever wanted to know how to figure out if a man was lying to you or about the information on his online dating profile or Facebook Wall? Have you ever wanted to know what really happened with the divorce that your man has been talking about or if the man you are dating is really in the midst of a divorce? Did you ever wonder what legal rights a mistresses has, such as does she need to hire an attorney once his wife finds out about the affair or is she legally entitled to an apology from her married man when he returns to his wife? If so, then Oh No He Didn't! is a must read for you!

Oh No He Didn't! is based on both my personal dating experiences and my professional legal experiences handling civil and criminal cases in the state and federal courts, including representing men criminally charged with physically assaulting women; representing women that sought restraining orders against their boyfriends/husbands to prevent further mental and physical abuse; representing men and women in contested and uncontested divorces; representing men in legitimation cases; and representing men and women in child custody, support, & visitation disputes.

I've been sharing my outrageous dating stories and legal advice with my family, friends, & clients for years. Now it's time for me to share them with the rest of the world.

DON'T ANSWER STATUS & BUGABOOS!

Before you start reading the 15 Outrageous Dating Experiences I must explain "Don't Answer Status" and "Bugaboos."

When I meet a man his name and telephone number are added to my cell phone address book. I never write his number down on a piece of paper and it is extremely rare that I memorize a man's telephone number. At most, I will memorize the area code of his telephone number if it isn't an Atlanta area code.

If a man has done something that makes me want to refrain from initiating any communication with him but his communications are still welcome, then his name and telephone number are simply deleted from my cell phone address book. This way there are no worries about my initiating any additional communications with him because I have no way to get in touch with him. Deleting his name and telephone number also prevents me from becoming a "Bugaboo." A Bugaboo is when you call or send too many text messages to someone in a short period of time and they either haven't responded to you or they respond to you with what else do you want. In essence you are bugging the hell out of them.

Now that I have explained Bugaboo it is back to the Don't Answer Status explanation. If after he has been deleted from my phone he calls, then only the telephone number is displayed and then I can let the call go to voicemail and check the message to return the call…or I can just return the call to the telephone number after I figure out whose number it is.

If he sends me a text message, then I generally know who it is based on the content of the text message. However, if I don't know who sent it, then I send a reply message asking who sent it without specifically stating that I don't know who it is. For example, I may send a "?" or I may send "who is asking?" After I figure out who it is, then I determine if I want to resume communicating with him. If I want to continue communicating with him, then his name is resaved in the address book. If not, his text message is simply ignored.

If a man has done something that makes me never want to communicate with him again (i.e. I don't have anything to say to him and I don't want to ever hear anything else he has to say), then his name is changed in my cell phone address book to Don't Answer. This way when he calls or sends a text message it displays in my phone as from Don't Answer. I have multiple entries listed in my cell phone address book as Don't Answer, so I have no clue who is trying to communicate with me and the communication is not answered.

Once a man's name is changed to Don't Answer it is never returned to his actual name. Every Christmas, New Year's and Valentine's Day I receive multiple well wishes from the Don't Answer's in my cell phone! Their communications are never answered!

OUTRAGEOUS DATING EXPERIENCE #1

Oh No He Didn't Send Me A Face Book Friend Request & He Was A Convicted Bank Robber!

In early 2009 my sister started telling me that I should get on Facebook because everyone was on it. She kept telling me that my cousins were on there and it was a great way to keep up with family members. For several months I ignored her suggestions that I join. A few months after her repeated suggestions that I join Facebook, I read an article that discussed the benefits of joining Facebook for business purposes. So I finally decided to get on Facebook. My user name for Facebook was AttorneyWright because I was planning to use it to promote my law firm services and events to my family and friends on Facebook.

ATTORNEY LISA D. WRIGHT

I kept my profile as simple as I could. Once my profile was setup I added my sisters, my cousins and my friends that I was currently in touch with. Then I added additional friends by searching for people that I was friends with from high school (Oak Park High, Oak Park, MI), undergrad (Kentucky State University), and graduate school (Duke University – The Fuqua School of Business and the Law School). I also received friend requests from friends and from some of my former law firm clients. I accepted the friend requests from friends and declined the friend requests from former clients because while I wanted to promote my business to my friends and family, I didn't want to use my Facebook account to promote my personal life to my former clients.

Lastly, I received some friend requests from people that I didn't recognize. For these friend requests I tried to figure out who they were and if I couldn't figure out who they were, then I usually just ignored their request. I should have stuck with this plan.

One day I received a friend request from a guy in Detroit that I thought I remembered from partying with during school breaks while I was in undergrad at Kentucky State University. ("Mr. Facebook"). From Mr. Facebook's friend request I sent him an email asking him how I knew him, was it from partying and hanging out back in the late '80s? Then I reviewed Mr. Facebook's profile and the majority of his pictures were from where he had attended Kappa Alpha Psi Fraternity, Inc. ("Kappa") events, which made me believe that he was one of the many Kappa men that I had partied with back in my younger days. So without confirming exactly how I knew him, I accepted Mr. Facebook's friend request.

In late July 2009, Mr. Facebook posted an update on his wall that he just started distance running. So, I posted a reply that I started distance running in March 2009 and I ran my first 10k in late June 2009. I started emailing Mr. Facebook beginner running tips. On August 9, 2009, my great-aunt passed away on her 94th birthday and I ended up having to plan a trip to Detroit to attend her funeral services. I sent Mr. Facebook an email that I was going to be in Detroit over the next weekend and maybe we could meet up and run in a 5k. Mr. Facebook said that would be great and asked me to see if I could find us an event. I found us a 5k race to run in Dearborn, MI.

Shortly thereafter, my lawyer brain actually decided to start acting like a lawyer! I thought to myself he never responded to my initial email about where do I know you from and who are you. So I sent him an email asking him exactly who he was, where he went to school, where he worked, etc. He responded with an extremely long email full of nothing! Ok, the email had a large number of words in it but it really didn't give me any great insights into exactly who he was and if he was someone really worth my time, but since I am into fitness I figured it would be nice to have some company on a 5k run.

The things I do recall about the email were: he was single, he had twin daughters that lived with their mother; he lived with his parents; his parents went to Wayne State University; his mother pledged Delta Sigma Theta Sorority, Inc. ("Delta") at Wayne State University (a few years after my Mother pledged Delta at Wayne State University); his father pledged Kappa at Wayne State University; he was currently in school at an online university and planned to transfer to Wayne State University where he wanted to pledge Kappa; he had previously owned his own restaurant that turned into an unsuccessful business venture; and he had lived with his ex-girlfriend and her children for several years but their relationship was over. I believe we traded a few more emails and then we exchanged phone numbers. We had approximately two telephone conversations before I arrived in Detroit.

I have lived in Atlanta since January 2000 and have never had a problem renting a car in Detroit before August 2009! I am not sure what was so special about the August 13-16, 2009 time period, but every rental car company at the airport was sold out of rental cars so I ended up having to get my girlfriend to pick me up at the airport and then having to share my sister's car for the weekend. I think this was God's blessing in disguise!

I told Mr. Facebook that I wasn't going to have a rental car for my time in Detroit, but I would be sharing my sister's car over the weekend. I flew to Detroit on Thursday, August 13, 2009. I sent Mr. Facebook a text message that I had arrived and made it to my sister's job so that I could share her car to get around town. He then sent me a text that said if I needed a ride to the race on Saturday, then one of his friend's could pick me up. Oh No He Didn't!

First of all, I didn't know Mr. Facebook well enough for him to pick me up to drive me to the race so why in the world would he think that I would want his friend to pick me up and drive me to the race? Second of all, I don't socialize with grown men that live in the Detroit metropolitan area that don't have a driver's license and a car! (Note: If you live in New York city or Chicago, or some other metropolitan areas where it is normal not to have a car, then I could socialize with you.)

So, I sent Mr. Facebook a text asking him what happened to his driver's license and car. Mr. Facebook responded that he didn't currently have a driver's license but he had paid his lawyer $6,500 so far and he only had another $1,500 left to pay so that he could get his license reinstated. Oh No He Didn't! I replied that I would just borrow my sister's car to get to the race.

After I got this text from Mr. Facebook I had to put my full legal research skills into action. I used to handle criminal law cases when I first opened my law firm so I knew that $8,000 in legal fees was for more than just a few speeding tickets or even a DUI (or two)! I could not wait to get home to my sister's to get on the internet to find out what crimes Mr. Facebook had committed to have accumulated $8,000 in legal fees.

When I got to my sister's around 10pm that evening the first website I went to was not working, the Michigan Department of Corrections – Offender Tracking Information System (http://www.state.mi.us/mdoc/asp/otis2.html). Since Mr. Facebook went to high school in Oakland County I figured I would check the criminal records in that county via the Court Explorer website (www.oakgov.com/circuit/). This is the Oakland County, Michigan Circuit Court website that lists civil and criminal court records on all cases that occurred in the county. I typed in Mr. Facebook's name and then the list of the criminal charges and what he had been convicted of appeared! The list that appeared was longer than the screen! I didn't print a copy of the list, but I remember that he had been convicted by a jury for possession of drugs and evading arrest, he was ordered to complete his GED and to serve 180 days in jail.

I was in shock! I was speechless! My sister was just laying there with me and we were both just staring at the screen and laughing. I told my sister to help me get my profile off Facebook immediately! My sister made one last effort to get me to stay on Facebook, but I totally ignored her! I wasn't interested in trying to just block Mr. Facebook from access to my profile, I wanted off of Facebook forever!!!!! My Facebook profile was removed on August 13, 2009 and has never been seen since! After I deleted my information from Facebook, Mr. Facebook never contacted me about running the race, or about anything else.

A few weeks after I got back to Atlanta I was bored one evening so I decided to check Mr. Facebook out on the Michigan Department of Corrections website. Mr. Facebook had also been convicted of bank robbery, armed robbery, and failure to pay child support.

Advice For Men:

- If you are a convicted felon, don't try to date an attorney.
- Don't try to associate yourself with a group that you are not a member of to make women think that you are a member of that group.

- If the woman you are planning to take on a date doesn't know your friend, then don't offer to have your friend pick her up for the date.

Advice For Women:

- Don't accept a Facebook friend request until you have confirmed the identity of the person making the friend request.
- Don't be afraid to reject a Facebook friend request from someone you don't know.
- Use your official State and county online criminal search internet websites to verify that the man you are about to meet is not a convicted criminal.
  - These websites generally provide the information for free and can be found with a simple web search, for example: Georgia judiciary criminal search.
  - The websites that appear with a .gov or a .us ending are the websites that are generally operated by the State or County offices that you will want to search.

OUTRAGEOUS DATING EXPERIENCE #2

Oh No He Didn't Tell Me If I Wasn't Taking His Calls, Then He Wasn't Taking My Calls... But He Kept Calling & Texting Anyway!

In December 2009 I was traveling for work to Washington, D.C. Normally, when I am traveling through airports I try to make sure that I have an attractive outfit on and makeup on because airports and planes are great places to meet new single men. As I was waiting at the gate to board the plane I noticed that the gate agent was checking me out. ("Mr. Airport"). So I made repeated eye contact with him. Shortly thereafter, he went on his lunch break and as I was sending text messages Mr. Airport asked if I would send him a text message. I said sure and I got Mr. Airport's telephone number. Mr. Airport said that he was in a bit of a rush because he was on his lunch break. I replied that I would send him a text with my contact information and then I boarded the plane. After I landed in Washington, D.C., I sent Mr. Airport a text and he requested that I give him a call while I was in route to my hotel.

After I got off the plane and I was waiting for the Metro train I gave Mr. Airport a call. We discussed the traditional get to know you conversation topics. Mr. Airport said he was single, no children, he was from the Midwest, lived in the Atlanta metropolitan area, and that he had more than enough siblings for a family baseball team.

When my train arrived I told Mr. Airport that I would have to end our call because I hated having long personal conversations on the train, but I would give him a call when I got settled in my hotel room. After I got to my hotel room, I went to the grocery store next door to get some food, returned to the hotel to eat dinner, sent several texts to my family and to the other men that I was dating, and then I gave Mr. Airport a call back. I can't even remember what we talked about. After we got off the phone I then turned my phone off for the evening and went to bed.

OH NO HE DIDN'T!

The next morning I received a text from Mr. Airport asking if I had dreamed about him. Truthfully, NO! But in the dating world, of course I did! So I responded to Mr. Airport that I dreamt of him all night long. Why in the world did he believe that? Because he is a man! So Mr. Airport responded with a text asking for the details about my dream! I told Mr. Airport that I wasn't going to tell him any details. Then Mr. Airport decided that my answer was not good enough for him so he kept asking me for details ALL DAY LONG! He repeatedly called and asked me for details and he repeatedly sent me text messages asking for details. I continued to tell him that I wasn't giving up any details. Mr. Airport had officially gotten on my last nerves and I hadn't even known him 24 hours! While he wasn't on Don't Answer Status yet, he was officially on Bugaboo Status! Thankfully, I was dating a few other men at the time so my focus was not on Mr. Airport at the time.

For the next few weeks Mr. Airport asked me to go out with him but I avoided it. I wasn't really that interested in dating him and I was busy dating others at the time. However, I managed to send him a text message every so often just to keep in touch.

ATTORNEY LISA D. WRIGHT

On January 14, 2010, I booked a plane ticket with the airline that Mr. Airport worked for to take a round trip flight from Atlanta to Dallas for the NBA All Star Basketball game, to travel on Sunday February 14, 2010 and to return on Monday, February 15, 2010. I was going to attend the game with my sister that lives in Detroit. I had purchased game tickets for us back in July, and we hadn't made our travel plans yet. So I told her that I booked my flight and the hotel for an excellent rate. Then she complained that she didn't want to go for just a one night trip. So I told her there was a 24-hour cancellation policy for my ticket so I would just cancel the original ticket and I would purchase another ticket leaving Atlanta on Saturday, February 13, 2010 and returning Monday, February 15, 2010.

So I went on the internet and purchased the new airline ticket leaving on Saturday February 13, 2010 and for what I thought was returning on Monday, February 15, 2010, with the price being a few dollars cheaper. I rebooked the hotel for the additional night and I thought we were all set for a fun filled weekend in Dallas. After I got all of our travel plans setup for the hotel and the rental car, then my sister could not locate her airline ticket voucher that she planned to use to pay for her plane ticket to Dallas. Well, she never found her airline ticket voucher before the time expired for me to cancel my airline ticket and I decided that I would go on the trip with or without out her!

A few days later she managed to find her airline ticket voucher; however, the airfares had increased substantially and were higher than the amount of her voucher. However, a few days later the airfares went down and she actually purchased her airline ticket to Dallas. I was thrilled at this point because the trip was finally coming together. Wrong!

On January 20, 2010, I logged onto the airline website to check my seats for an upcoming work flight to Washington, D.C. The airline website listed all of my upcoming flights: the flights to and from Washington, D.C. and the flights to and from Dallas. However, there was a problem with the flight from Dallas: it said that I had over 50 days until departure…which meant that I booked it for a March 15 return date instead of a February 15 return date!

How could this have happened? Well when I booked the original ticket the airline pop-up calendar initially popped up with March and I had to force it back into

February , which I apparently didn't do the second time when I booked the second ticket; and because the calendar days for February and March are the same I didn't notice the difference when I selected the return flight on the second ticket.

Initially I tried to correct the problem on the website but they wanted $340 to change the return flight and I wasn't paying that much to fix it when the entire ticket only cost me $229. Then I checked the one-way ticket price and it was only $142, so there was no way I was paying $340 to resolve the problem. Next, I called the airline and tried to get them to fix it for me without a fee. However, the first person that I spoke with told me that it would be $150 plus the difference in the airfare to change it. Not! I asked to speak with a supervisor. He got his supervisor on the phone and his supervisor told me that he would only charge me $150. Not! I told the supervisor that the one way fare was only $142 and the supervisor told me that I should go ahead and purchase the one way ticket. I hung up on both of them. Over the next few weeks I tried several other options and I didn't like any of them because none of them were free.

So, I decided that I would get Mr. Airport's opinion on the situation. Note: I didn't say that I was going to ask him to change it for me. I sent him a text message explaining the situation and asked him if he had any suggestions for me to get it resolved. Mr. Airport told me send me your ticket number and I will take care of getting it changed for you when I go to work next weekend. Mr. Airport told me that I would also owe him for doing this, at least a hug and a kiss. I told him ok, but I said to myself I should have just paid that $142 back in January and purchased the one way ticket.

But with less than two weeks left to go before my trip to Dallas, I sent Mr. Airport a text with all of the information regarding my original ticket and with all of the information regarding my desired return. I thought that the change I needed was extremely simple. I simply needed to return to Atlanta on Monday, February 15, 2010 instead of Monday, March 15, 2010 and I didn't care what time of day that I flew back because I was just trying to get home in February instead of March. But who am I to think that things are simple?

After I sent Mr. Airport the text with my flight information I didn't get a reply from him. So, a few hours later I sent a second text asking if he got the information. However, he didn't reply to my second text either which I thought was odd because he was frequently on Bugaboo Status with respect to my lack of communication with him.

Since I didn't hear back from Mr. Airport regarding his receipt of my flight information and I didn't want to get on Bugaboo Status with him, I figured I would just keep checking my itinerary on the airline website to see when it was changed. I checked my itinerary on Friday, no change. I checked my itinerary at least three times on Saturday, no change. I checked my itinerary on Super bowl Sunday at least two times before the football game started, no change.

Then when I was on the way home from a not so great Super bowl party and I received a voice mail message from Mr. Airport that my ticket had been changed. I was thrilled, this definitely made up for the disappointing Super bowl party. Mr. Airport's message included my new flight number and the seat assignment, which was exactly the same as the original March 15th flight. I found it a bit too coincidental that he was able to get me on the same flight with the same seat assignment as the original flight, but I wasn't going to complain about it. After I got his voice message I gave him a call and we chatted for a while as I was driving home. After I got home I went on the internet to pull up the airline itinerary but it still had my return flight as March 15.

On Monday morning when I got to work I went on the airline website and pulled up the itinerary and it still showed that I was returning on March 15. I called my work travel agency to find out if they could pull up the reservation to see if they were showing the February 15 return date; however, they could not access the reservation and the airline would not provide them with any information regarding my reservation because I had booked the reservation on the internet. I sent Mr. Airport a text message that the reservation still showed a March 15 return date; however, he never responded.

When I got home from work I called the airline to ask if my reservation had been changed and it just wasn't showing on the internet itinerary, they said no. I asked if any changes had been made to the reservation over the weekend and they said no. I asked the airline representative how much it would cost to get the reservation changed (after I explained the mistake that I made when I booked the ticket); she replied it would be $1,100. I told her that I would not be going to Dallas for the weekend and I would use the ticket toward another trip in the future.

I called my sister to tell her that I wasn't going to Dallas because Mr. Airport hadn't changed my ticket and I wasn't going to spend $1,100 to get my return flight changed. My sister told me to forward her my information regarding my ticket and she would call the airline and try to get the return flight changed for me. I then turned my cell phone off for several hours so that I could peacefully try to figure out a cheaper way to get home from Dallas. I was on the internet looking at buying a one way ticket home from Dallas, which was now about $350 and I wouldn't get back to Atlanta until after 9pm; I was also on the internet looking at buying an airline ticket that would connect thru Atlanta and then I could just not get on the connecting flight; and I was considering driving the rental car home from Dallas, which would have been an eleven hour drive home. I wasn't thrilled with any of these options.

Around 11:30pm I decided to turn my cell phone back on to purchase the one way ticket to Atlanta. However, I had a text from my sister that she had gotten the ticket changed and for me to go on the internet to verify that my itinerary had been changed. I immediately turned my computer on and checked. My return flight had finally been changed to February 15, 2010! I called her and she said she explained what happened to the internet based customer service representatives and they changed the return flight with no charge.

Tuesday morning when I got to work I printed out my updated travel itinerary and I was looking forward to my trip to Dallas at the end of the week. After I got off work I stopped at Dillard's to check out some makeup items that I was considering purchasing for the trip. While I was at Dillard's I got a text message from a Don't Answer that said send me your conf number. I was so totally confused with the "conf number" because initially I was thinking that this was regarding a conference call from work and I don't put work calls on Don't Answer Status. After a few minutes of thinking about it, I realized that this was a text from Mr. Airport asking me to send him my airline ticket confirmation number. Normally, I don't respond to any calls or text messages that I get from men on Don't Answer Status, but this time was an exception. I didn't actually save the text but in summary I told him that I didn't need his kind of help and I had absolutely nothing else left to say to him. I was hoping that this was the end of him. However, it wasn't!

As I was driving home from Dillard's I was on the phone with a friend of mine, and he called from a number that displayed as Unknown Caller. I answered the call and as soon as I recognized his voice I hung up on him. Then he called right back and I refused to answer the call. He left a voice mail message with a bunch of nonsense and at the end of the nonsense he said that since I was not taking his calls he would not be taking my calls. Great, this is exactly what I wanted!

Then about twenty minutes later I got another call, but from an area code I didn't recognize. I just let that call go to voice mail as well. I actually thought that it was a call from him, but it wasn't. This message was from his coworker that was actually the person that was supposed to have made the change to the ticket. She said that when she pulled up the ticket she didn't see anything that needed to be changed, so she didn't change anything. How stupid! Then she told me don't worry about a thing, just go to the airport on Friday and she would make sure that the return flight was changed when she got to work on the weekend. Yeah right!

Approximately twenty minutes later Mr. Airport left me another voice mail message with more nonsense and at the end of the nonsense he said "I won't ever call you." Now, I considered this message a blessing that I would never have to hear from Mr. Airport again!

Then, thirty minutes later I received a text message from him. And then within less than an hour I got another text message from him. I had to turn my phone off for a few hours because I was sick of receiving text messages from him. I prayed that he would eventually stop calling and texting.

As luck would have it, I ended up not even going to Dallas because there was a winter snow storm that Thursday that started in Dallas and then moved across the country to Atlanta. My original flight was cancelled due to the storm. I contacted the airline to verify that my flight was actually cancelled due to the weather and not because of Mr. Airport. The airline confirmed that the flight was cancelled due to the weather. After six hours of trying to get confirmed on another flight, I was finally confirmed on another flight; however, that flight was also cancelled due to the winter storm.

My sister ended up going to Dallas because her flight from Detroit wasn't cancelled. She also attended the NBA All Star game without me. I had to watch the game from home on television.

My prayers that Mr. Airport would stop calling and texting me were answered for a brief 10 days! On February 18, 2010, Mr. Airport sent me the following text message: "Hey! U still want me to go to HELL?" While I didn't send Mr. Airport a reply, my answer is YES!

Please note that the only reason I even took the time to figure out which Don't Answer sent me this text is because I was writing this book. I forwarded the text to my email account and then the forwarded text message displays the originating telephone number and then I determined that it was from him.

Advice for Men:

- Don't tell a woman that you will never call her again and then continue calling and texting her.

- Don't volunteer to perform tasks for a woman that you know you don't have the skills to perform.

- If you tell a woman that you have completed something for her with the assistance of someone else, then make sure that your assistant is competent to assist you in getting the job done AND that the job was done BEFORE you tell the woman that you have completed the task for her.

Advice for Women:

- If you know that you are not interested in getting to know a man any further, then put him on Don't Answer Status as soon as possible.

- If you delay putting a man on Don't Answer Status because you think that the things he does that irritate you won't bother you over time, then you are kidding yourself as long as you continue dating him.

OUTRAGEOUS DATING EXPERIENCE #3

Oh No He Didn't Confirm At 6:15PM That We Were Going Out At 7:30PM & Then Try to Reschedule At 7:15PM!

On January 28, 2010, as I was leaving the building where I live heading to the Gucci store at Phipps Mall I met a gentleman that lives in my building. ("Mr. Neighbor"). As I was rushing out of the elevator to the parking garage lobby we engaged in a brief conversation, I gave him my number, and told him to send me a text message with his contact information. I was trying to get to the Gucci store before they closed because a keychain that I wanted had just come in (I was purchasing it with the last of a 2009 Christmas gift card) and I was also in a hurry because my dinner date didn't know that I was making a stop at the Gucci store before I was meeting him.

Mr. Neighbor sent me a text with his contact information, including his name and phone number while I was driving to the Gucci store at Phipps Plaza. The next day we exchanged a few introductory text messages, my usual tell me some information about you questions. Of course I don't remember everything that he sent in the text messages, but I do recall that he said he was single, he had a one year old daughter, he worked from home, he was working on writing a book, and he was in his early thirties. I immediately told him that I wasn't currently interested in dating anyone with kids, a wife, or an ex-wife because I had recently had more than my fair share of dating men in those situations. Mr. Neighbor said to give him a chance because he was a good father to his daughter, he wasn't looking for a mother for his daughter, and he just wanted some companionship. I said fair enough, but I had given him my full disclosure up front.

We continued communicating via text messages because I had no real interest in talking to him on the phone after he said he had a child. Mr. Neighbor would ask me on the spur of the moment if I wanted to meet up and I would find an excuse to decline his invitation. Honestly, I wasn't really interested in him and I wasn't interested in just meeting up with him at the drop of a dime. However, I would periodically tell myself to give him a chance.

One evening he suggested that we meet in our building's social room for a glass of wine and to chat. I finally agreed to this "spur of the moment" date. However, I said that I needed an hour before I could meet him in the social room. I had to get my mind in the right social mood and I had to take a shower and get dressed. We agreed to meet, or so I thought. An hour later I went down to the social room. When I got to the room there were several other residents in the room watching the Grammy's and it was pretty loud, but I said that I would endure the loud party atmosphere so that I could socialize with Mr. Neighbor. I waited in the social room for Mr. Neighbor for about 15 minutes and then I sent him a text message asking him where he was at. He responded that he was at Wal-Mart. Oh No He Didn't! I should have put Mr. Neighbor on Don't Answer Status that night!

But I thought to myself maybe there was a miscommunication regarding our meeting that evening and I decided to give him one more chance. I sent him a text message regarding our failed meeting. I told him that we would no longer be attempting to setup a first social event on a spur of the moment basis (i.e. bootleg), we would plan a date for a specific time and then we would go on that date as planned.

So a few days later, we tried to meet up for drinks. However, that plan didn't work either because initially when he asked if I was available to meet I was, but then a guy that I dated a few years ago (that had never been put on Don't Answer Status) wanted to hang out, so I decided I would rather spend the evening having fun with my single, handsome, and childless friend. I asked Mr. Neighbor if we could meet for drinks on Thursday evening, to which he said he couldn't because he was flying to California and he would be gone for a week. So we ended up planning to go out the following Wednesday for dinner.

The next morning I sent Mr. Neighbor a text telling him to have a safe trip to California. Then at around 1 p.m., Mr. Neighbor informed me that his trip to California was delayed until Friday, so I asked him if he was available to go to dinner that evening around 7pm or 7:30pm. Mr. Neighbor said that he was available and we confirmed our dinner date for the evening.

Around 6:15pm, I got a text from Mr. Neighbor asking if we were still going to dinner at 7:30pm. I replied yes. After I sent him my reply I set my alarm clock so that I could get a cat nap and then I could get up and get ready for our date. At 7:00pm I got up and started getting ready, got dressed, and put my makeup on. Then I walked back into my bedroom where my cell phone was and I happened to see that my text message light was blinking. There was a text message from Mr. Neighbor that I received at 7:15pm that asked if we could push our date back to 8:30pm because he wanted to finish packing for his trip. Oh No He Didn't! And my answer was hell no!

However, I sent him the following text message: We will never b going out or meeting up etc. I don't do bootleg. Sun nite when u said let's meet in the building social room I went down there @ time I said I'd b there n u were @ walmart. How many hrs 2day did u have 2 prepare 4 7 or 730? Did u not send me a text followup askn if 730 was stil good? Then u cum up w dumb azz request 4 830! Meet up w the next female @ 830 cause I'm not the one!

He sent me the following text message in response: It was really some money shit... N I'm done now.. I can tell ur feisty n ur used to havin yr way n I can cater to u but money first I didn't try to stand u up.

Mr. Neighbor was put on Don't Answer Status immediately. Does he really think that I believe his "money shit" excuse? Does he really think that I was concerned that he was trying to stand me up? If a man was going to stand me up, then he wouldn't send me a text asking me to change the meeting time. Standing someone up means not showing up at the agreed upon time and not calling to explain that you will be late or that you won't be attending the date. Lastly, what does wanting to have a man cater to me have to do with his complete lack of respect for me or my time? I want a man to cater to me AND respect my time!

On February 7th he sent a text that he really did want to take me out. I didn't reply. On February 8th he sent a text asking if the "ice started to thaw out yet." I didn't reply. Then on February 18th he sent another text asking how I was doing. I didn't reply. He also sent another text message in March 15th. I didn't reply.

I would be doing much better if he would stop texting, but that is the beauty of Don't Answer Status. I never have to answer. This book is the only reason that I have continued tracking the identity of the men placed on Don't Answer Status. Just in case Mr. Neighbor is reading this book, the ice has not thawed, I am doing great, and I have no plans on ever going out on any dates with you.

Advice for Men:

- If you don't have the money to pay for a date an hour before the date, then don't confirm the date an hour before the date.
- When you don't have the money to pay for a specific type of date, then don't try to take a woman on that type of date.
- Take your date on the type of date that you can afford, but don't make it look like you are a cheapskate.

Advice for Women:

- Your time is valuable. If a man doesn't respect your time for a first date, then don't go out with him because he will never learn to respect your time in the future.

- Once you have put a man on Don't Answer Status, leave him on Don't Answer Status, even if he sends you texts daily.

- If you are not interested in dating a man with children, then don't be afraid to tell him that you are not interested in dating a man that already has children. In the event that you are reluctant to say this to him directly, then you have two options: you can send it to him via text message or you can show him a copy of this advice. I am sure that he will get the message. If he doesn't get the message when you show him this page of the book, then tell him to send me an email at attorney@lisadwright.com and I will tell him for you.

OUTRAGEOUS DATING EXPERIENCE #4

Oh No He Didn't Force Me To File A Police Report Against Him!

One Saturday at the end of July 2008, after I returned from a week long traveling summer vacation, I went to the Target Store at Atlantic Station. It was just a regular Saturday visit to target for groceries and toiletries. As I was shopping for groceries I noticed a gentleman wearing a "unique" denim outfit and he was talking on his cell phone trying to sound important. I actually noticed him several times because it seemed as if he was in almost every grocery aisle that I was in. After he got off the phone he managed to start a conversation with me while we were near the dairy section. We had a five minute conversation, we exchanged business cards, and I continued with my shopping. After I got all of the items I needed I proceeded to the checkout line.

Then I paid for all of my items and headed for the elevators (to enter and exit this Target you have to either take the elevator or the escalator down to the exit) and I noticed that he was standing at the elevator looking like he was waiting for me. ("Mr. Harasser").

I was right; Mr. Harasser was waiting for me to arrive at the elevator so that he could continue talking with me while I was leaving the store. Mr. Harasser asked me when he would hear from me after we left Target. I told Mr. Harasser that he would hear from me when he called me. Mr. Harasser asked me why I wasn't going to call him first. I told Mr. Harasser that I don't initiate the first communication with a man after I meet him, I allow the man to initiate the initial communication if he wants to continue communicating with me. Mr. Harasser didn't like this response and wanted to have a debate with me about it. Now most people think that I just love debating because I am an attorney, but I actually hate debating. I prefer to say what I have to say once and you can agree with it or not. I am generally not going to change my mind based on what you have to say and I definitely wasn't going to change my mind about my dating strategies for communicating with men based on my conversation with Mr. Harasser, but he wanted to keep on trying.

Unfortunately, I had to ride in the Target elevator with Mr. Harasser talking to me the entire time. He kept asking me why I wouldn't call him first. I kept telling him that I would not be calling him first and that there was nothing else to talk about. After I got out of the elevator Mr. Harasser continued talking to me as I walked to my car and put my bags into the car. By the time I got my bags into the car I was sick of him and so not interested in him that I had to literally push him out of the way to get into my car. As I was trying to close my car door to get away from him (and his voice) I told him that I wasn't interested in him and I told him that he didn't need to call me. Then I closed my car door, I put the car in reverse (so that the car doors would lock), and I thought that I was done with him.

However, he called me within thirty seconds of when I drove out of the Target parking lot. He apologized and said that I must have taken him the wrong way and he wanted to get to know me. I told him as nicely as I could that I was not interested in getting to know him and I would appreciate it if he would not call me anymore. I told him that I was ending the call and then I hung up. He called back at least two more times while I was in the car, but I didn't answer. I immediately added his name to the address book in my cell phone as Don't Answer.

Sunday arrived and it was the last official day of my vacation and I wanted to try and enjoy it by resting at home all day. Around noon I got a text message from a telephone number that wasn't in my address book, I opened it up and there was a picture of an African American man's penis, in other words a pornographic penis picture. Because I didn't know who sent me the text I could only speculate that Mr. Harasser sent me this picture. About five minutes later I got another text message from the same telephone number with a second pornographic penis picture. (At this point you may be asking yourself, as everyone asked me, was it a picture of Mr. Harasser's penis…well I can't answer that question because I never saw his penis so I don't know if the penis in the picture was his or not).

After receiving two unwanted pornographic penis pictures on my phone I had to use my attorney research tools to confirm that it was Mr. Harasser that was sending me these pornographic text messages. I went online to access

Westlaw's attorney research database to reverse look-up the telephone number that was sending the penis pictures to confirm that Mr. Harasser was sending them. Mr. Harasser was indeed the person that was sending me the penis pictures.

I then sent Mr. Harasser a text message that said I know that you are sending me these text messages, I included his name in the text message. I also told him to stop sending me pornographic pictures on my cell phone and if he did not stop sending me pornographic pictures, then I would report him to the police. Five minutes later he sent me another text message with an oral sex pornographic picture. Then five minutes later he sent a fourth pornographic picture.

I guess Mr. Harasser thought I was joking when I told him that I was going to report him to the police. I made sure that every text message from him was saved in my phone before I got showered and dressed to go to the police station. Then I called my sister and told her all about meeting Mr. Harasser, the pornographic text messages he sent me, and that I was on the way to report his ass to the police. I told her that I was forwarding all of the messages to her in case something happened to my phone. I told her that she didn't have to open them if she didn't want to but I wanted to make sure that she had the files as a backup for me. I then forwarded all of the pictures to her. Then I got dressed and headed out to report Mr. Harasser to local law enforcement.

Initially I tried to get a criminal warrant filed at the Fulton County Courthouse. However, the Courthouse was closed. So, I went to the City of Atlanta Police Station to file a police report. Initially I spoke with the officer that was sitting at the front desk. I provided a brief overview of the situation and then showed him the pictures that were on my phone. He was shocked and immediately telephoned an officer from the back to take my report. A female police officer came out to the lobby area take the report. I gave her the details of meeting Mr. Harasser, I gave her the business card he gave me, then I gave her my cell phone and showed her the text message pornographic pictures that I had received and she was totally shocked. She was shocked by the fact that this man sent these pictures to me when I had known him for less than 24 hours.

I also spoke with at least two other male police officers about Mr. Harasser. One male officer asked me how

I knew after just ten minutes that I wasn't interested in Mr. Harasser. I told him that it doesn't take long for me to know that I am not interest in someone and that Mr. Harasser's actions fully supported my ten minute assessment of him. The male police officers were shocked that Mr. Harasser sent me those pornographic pictures and they both asked me if the pictures were of Mr. Harasser's penis. I had to tell both officers that I had not gotten to know Mr. Harasser on that level so I had no idea whether or not the penis in the pictures was Mr. Harasser's.

I was at the police station for over an hour. This was the first time I had ever had to file a police report against anyone in my life. I felt like I was left with no other choice but to file a police report. I wasn't jumping for joy after filing the report, but I felt a better sense of security after getting it filed. The last police officer that I spoke with told me that they would contact Mr. Harasser regarding my report and instruct him to leave me alone. I prayed that they would contact Mr. Harasser and that a call (or visit) from the police would finally get him to leave me alone so that I could posslbly enjoy the rest of my last afternoon of my summer 2008 vacation.

I am confident that the City of Atlanta Police contacted Mr. Harasser and instructed him not to contact me any further because Mr. Harasser never contacted me again. Mr. Harasser never sent me any more pornographic text messages. Of course both of Mr. Harasser's telephone numbers are on Don't Answer Status in my phone.

Advice for Men:

- Don't send text messages with pornographic pictures to women that are not interested in dating you.
- Don't let your male ego put you in a position of having to defend yourself in a criminal proceeding for harassing a woman that you barely even know because your feelings are hurt that she is not interested in dating you.
- If a woman specifically tells you that she is not interested in getting to know you, then believe her and move on to meeting the next woman.

Advice for Women:

- If you have asked a man nicely to stop communicating with you and he then starts harassing you, then make sure you save all text messages, photos, emails, etc. from him so that you will have the documentation to report it to the police.

- If you are getting harassed by a man, then don't be afraid to report him to local law enforcement. Don't try to take matters into your own hands.

- If you receive harassing or threatening communications from a man, make sure that you tell at least one family member or friend about it so that if something happens, you will have a witness to your situation if it becomes necessary in the future.

ATTORNEY LISA D. WRIGHT

INCIDENT REPORT

Prepared: 7/26/2008 9:21:07 PM

Incident #: 08█████████00

Workflow Status: Report Approved by Central Records

Incident Info

Incident #	Report Date	Time	Date Occurred	Time	Poss. Date	Time	Beat
08████-00	7/27/2008	1600	7/26/2008	1730	7/27/2008	1430	501

Shift	Zone	Location			Location Type	Rpt. District	Rpt. Officer	Inv. Officer
E	05	1380 ATLANTIC DRIVE			24	501		4341

Children Inv.	Family Inv.	Gang Related	Prev. Complaints	Prior Court Orders	Disposition	Dispo. Date	Time
	2						

How Committed

VICTIM WAS RECEIVING HARRASSING PHONE CALLS FROM SUBJECT THAT SHE MET AT TARGET

Reason No Arrest	Relationship of Parties	Weather
		1

Offenses

	Offense	Offense					# of Victims
1	1316	TERRORISTIC THREAT/INTIMI					1
	IBR Code	Att/Comp	UCR	UCR Arson	UCR Status	Bias Incident	Method of Entry	Family Violence
	1316	C	2600		I			N

Involved Parties

	Name Type	Name
1	VICTIM	WRIGHT, DIONNE LISA

Address		Bldg.	Apt. #	Home Phone
████████, ATL, GA ████			███	

DOB	Age	DL Number	DL State	DL Expire	Sex	Race	Height	Weight	Hair	Eyes
██████	████	████	GA	████	F	B				

Hair Style	Hair Type	Facial Hair	Complexion

Appear	Speech	Hand	Gloves	Teeth	Glasses	Hat	Mask	Eye Defect	Skin Tone Type	Clothing Type

Body Markings Type	Body Markings Description

SSN	Occupation	GCIC Code

Employer	Employer Address	Work Phone	Wk. Ext.

	INCIDENT REPORT	Prepared:
	Incident #: 08-███████-00	7/28/2008 9:21:07 PM

Suspects

Name Type						Name					
SUSPECT						███████					
Address					Bldg.		Apt. #		Home Phone		
██████, ATL, GA ████									████████		
DOB	Age	DL Number	DL State	DL Expire		Sex	Race	Height	Weight	Hair	Eyes
						M	██				
Hair Style			Hair Type			Facial Hair			Complexion		
Appear	Speech	Hand	Gloves	Teeth	Glasses	Hat	Mask	Eye Defect	Skin Tone Type	Clothing Type	
SSN		Occupation									
Employer		Employer Address						Work Phone		Wk. Ext.	
Body Markings Type		Body Markings Description									

No Arrests to Display!

No Vehicles to Display!

No Property to Display!

Narrative

ON THE ABOVE LISTED DATE AND TIME, MS LISA DIONNE WRIGHT CAME INTO THE PRECINCT LOCATED AT 220 SPRING ST TO REQUEST A REPORT. MS WRIGHT STATED THAT SHE MET A GUY KNOWN AS ████████ ON 07/26/2008 AT THE TARGET LOCATED INSIDE 1380 ATLANTIC DRIVE (ATLANTIC STATION) AROUND 1730 HRS. MS WRIGHT STATED THAT THEY TALKED FOR A FEW MINUTES AND EXCHANGED PHONE NUMBERS. MS WRIGHT STATED THAT AS SHE CONTINUED TO TALK WITH MR ████████ SHE KNEW THERE WAS NO INTEREST AND ASKED IF HE WOULD NOT CONTACT HER. MR ████████ INSISTED THAT THEY TALK AND CALLED MS WRIGHT. ONCE MS WRIGHT RECEIVED THE PHONE CALL FROM MR ████████ SHE ASKED IF HE COULD STOP CALLING AND TOLD HIM THAT SHE WASNT INTERESTED IN TALKING WITH HIM ANY LONGER. MR ████████ THEN BEGUN TO SEND MS WRIGHT OBSCENE PICTURES SHOWING THE GENITAL AREA OF A MALE AND OBSCENE PICTURES OF SEX SCENES. MS WRIGHT STATED THAT SHE RECEIVED 6 MESSAGES FROM 1150 HRS ON 07/27/2008 UNTIL 1430 HRS ON 07/27/2008. MS WRIGHT STATED THAT ONCE SHE SENT HIM A MESSAGE STATING FOR HIM TO STOP OR SHE WOULD PURSUE LEGAL ACTION, THEN HE SENT 4 ADDITIONAL OBSCENE PICTURES. MS WRIGHT STATED THAT SHE MADE IT VERY CLEAR TO MR ████████ THAT HE WASNT INTERESTED IN TALKING WITH HIM AND I ASKED FOR HIM TO STOP.

THE UNDERSIGNED, BEING DULY SWORN, UPON HIS OR HER OATH, DEPOSES AND STATES THAT THE FOREGOING IS TRUE, CORRECT, COMPLETE AND LEGIBLE TO THE BEST OF HIS/HER KNOWLEDGE AND BELIEF.

Reporting Officer (Elec. Sig.)	ID #	Assignment	Gender	Signed Date
██████ (YES)	██	██		7/28/2008
Supervisor (Elec. Sig.)	ID #	Assignment	Gender	Signed Date
██████ (YES)	██	██		7/28/2008

Incident #: ████████-00

Page 2 of 3

ATTORNEY LISA D. WRIGHT

INCIDENT REPORT

Incident #: 08⬛⬛⬛-00

Prepared:

7/28/2008 9:21:07 PM

Clerk ID # 2427

File Date 7/28/2008 9:21:04 PM

54

OUTRAGEOUS DATING EXPERIENCE #5

Oh No He Didn't Tell Me He Was Celibate With An Oral Sex Disclaimer!

I am a female that loves professional football, so I often get season tickets to the Atlanta Falcons games. My first set of Falcons season tickets was in 2001, the year Michael Vick was drafted by the Falcons. I continued to get Falcons season tickets off and on over the years. Most years that I have had season tickets I have had a great social life with attending the games and then dating the men that I have met at the games.

For the 2009 Falcons season, I had a plan that I would get the cheapest available season tickets so that I could attend the games and get the maximum social benefits at the lowest possible price. However, this plan didn't initially work liked I had planned. I thought that with any ticket to get into the Georgia Dome I would be able to get on the 100 level (i.e. the main level for socializing), but I was wrong! I found out that I didn't have access to the 100 level when I got to the first pre-season game and I was denied access to the 100 level, they told me that I couldn't get on the 100 level with my 300 level ticket.

In all of the prior years I either had a 100 level ticket or a club level ticket, so I had no clue that I wouldn't be able to get on the 100 level at the Georgia Dome with my 300 level ticket.

The next business day after I attended the pre-season game I called my Falcons Season Ticket Sales Representative and asked if I could purchase an upgraded 100 level ticket and he told me that I couldn't because they were already sold out. So I would just have to keep my 300 level tickets and do some maneuvering for the rest of the season to maximize my social experience. I just had to find someone with a 100 level ticket to let me borrow their ticket to get on the 100 level and then I would be ready to get my full Falcons game socializing on…which is exactly what I did for the rest of the season.

OH NO HE DIDN'T!

On October 18, 2009, I was looking forward to the Atlanta Falcons versus the Chicago Bears Sunday night game. I generally planned out my game day outfits a few hours before the game (i.e. so that I would look my best to maximize my socializing opportunities on the way to the game and at the game). On this Sunday I decided to wear my new Express perfectly fitted blue jeans, my cropped grey and silver sweater from Express, my silver Gucci necklace with my favorite silver Gucci evening bag, my large silver hoop earrings, and my black Donald Pliner with medium height heel shoe boots. About an hour and a half before the game I started getting ready. I got my hair, MAC makeup (Studio Tech foundation and Dazzleglass) and outfit perfect for socializing at the game, and by 7:45 pm I was finally ready to get to the Dome!

Since I live in downtown Atlanta taking the MARTA train to the Falcons game was pretty convenient. I walked from my building to the Civic Center train station. It was a bit chilly out that night, so I was glad that I didn't have to walk too far and that I didn't have to wait long for the train. As soon as I got to the waiting area for the train, the train pulled up.

Within a minute of getting on the train a gentleman asked if I wanted to sit next to him. I gave him a quick glance, thought he was cute, and then decided that I would like to sit next to him. After I sat down he asked me if I was going to the game and if I was going to the game alone. I replied that I was going to the game and that my girlfriend that I had season tickets with was meeting me at the Georgia Dome. He was on the train with a friend, and I assumed that he was attending the game with him (but I later found out that my assumption was wrong).

While we were on the train I asked him where his seats were in the Georgia Dome and he replied that his seats were on the 100 level. Perfect! I then told him that my seat was on the 300 level and asked if he could get me on the 100 level at half-time. He told me he would be happy to get me on the 100 level! I said to myself what a perfect way to start the evening and I wasn't even at the Georgia Dome yet. We exchanged telephone numbers before we got to the Georgia Dome and continued our conversation until after we got off the train and we got to the doors of Georgia Dome. We said goodbye and I left him to meet up with my friend for the start of the game.

During the first half of the game we exchanged several text messages about each other and about the game. I am unsure as to how many text messages we actually sent because I have been known to send an excessive amount of text messages during NFL games to men that I meet immediately before the game starts (LOL). He sent several text messages asking me to send a picture of my girlfriend because his friend that he was with at the game wanted to see what she looked like and possibly meet her at half-time. However, my girlfriend and I kept telling him that we were not sending any pictures. Additionally, I told my girlfriend that I saw his friend on the train and he was not cute so she would more than likely not be interested in meeting him.

Half-time finally arrived! So we exchanged text messages regarding where to meet so that he could get us onto the 100 level. However, when we made the plan to meet up we didn't realize that we were on opposite ends of the Georgia Dome and it would take him much longer to get through the major crowds on the 100 level to make it to our designated meeting location. So, my girlfriend and I got down to the 100 level pretty quickly and waited for what seemed like an eternity for him to meet us. We got tired of waiting for him and we decided to head back up to our seats for the start of the second half. And as luck would have it, as soon as we started heading back up to the 300 level he sent a text that he was waiting for us. I decided that I was going back down to meet up with him, but my girlfriend decided she was going back to our 300 level seats. Oh well, I wasn't missing out on a good social opportunity because my girlfriend wanted to go back to the top of the Georgia Dome.

I made it to where he was waiting, he gave me a hug and passed me his ticket so that I could show it to the usher to get into the 100 level seating area. Then he attempted to get one last beer, but because it was a Sunday night game they stopped serving alcohol at the end of half-time. (Normally for Sunday afternoon games they stop selling beer and alcohol at the end of the third quarter.) Even though he couldn't get a beer he got me some refreshments and then we headed to his seats. His seats were MUCH better than mine, despite the fact that they were end-zone seats. We were right on top of the football action. Then, to my surprise the friend that he was sitting with at the game was not the guy that he was on the train with. The friend that he was sitting with at the game was fine as hell! (Friend, if you are reading this book and you have figured out who you are, then feel free to send me an email). I sent my girlfriend a text with this updated cute friend information and told her she should strongly reconsider joining us on the 100 level, but she chose to stay in our 300 level seats.

After my brief text to my girlfriend I resumed my conversation with my new male friend. We continued our getting to know each other conversation while enjoying the Falcons game. He told me he was single (never married), no children, where he was originally from, how many siblings he had, how long he had lived in Atlanta, his age (early 30s), where he completed his undergraduate education, where he completed his graduate education, where he worked full-time (in finance for a cellular communications company), where he worked part-time (referee), and what fraternity he was in (Kappa). Then he told me that he was celibate and had been for a few years. ("Mr. Celibate"). So I responded that that was cool. Mr. Celibate said that he had been celibate for about three years because he felt that sex had become too big of a focus in his prior relationships. Mr. Celibate said that sometimes women didn't understand that he was celibate and that some women had taken offense to this. I told Mr.

Celibate that his celibacy didn't bother me at all. Now while it didn't bother me, I was a bit shocked that we were having this conversation at the Falcons football game. However, if Mr. Celibate wanted to get that conversation taken care of early on, then that was fine with me. We continued talking and enjoying the game. The Falcons won!

After the game ended we left the Georgia Dome together to catch the MARTA train. By the time the game was over the temperature had dropped and I was freezing. Mr. Celibate let me use his jacket to keep warm. While we were on the first train we held hands. Then we got off the first train at the Five Points station to transfer to the second train. As we were waiting for the second train we were hugging so that he could keep me warm. However, he was trying to warm my butt with his hands. He started this process by placing his hands in my back pockets and then he moved his hands from inside my jean pockets to inside my jeans, all while his jacket was hanging (i.e. covering) my butt. Then he wanted to have a discussion about the type of panty that I had on. I told him I had on a thong. Mr. Celibate told me I had on a g-string. We debated the issue for about five minutes and then I told Mr. Celibate that I would let him win the debate and he was the official panty expert.

I thought Mr. Celibate being all touchy feely with my ass and then debating what type of undergarment I had on was extremely odd for a man that just told me that he was celibate because most people that I know (or have known) that are celibate avoid situations that may incite sexual excitement....and I could definitely tell he was getting excited.

By the time we got on the second train Mr. Celibate asked me if he could spend the night. Oh No He Didn't! HELL NO! Mr. Celibate begged me to spend the night, but I repeatedly refused! So he reluctantly just agreed to get off the train with me at my stop for a good night kiss and hug, and then he got on the next train so that he could continue his train ride home. I sent him a text when I got inside to let him know that I made it inside safely, what a night. I told him to call me when he made it to his car.

Of course he called me when he got to his car and then we talked from the time he got into his car until he got home, and continued talking after he got home. We were on the phone for over an hour. We talked about a variety of subjects, we got along pretty well. However, he did ask me several times why I would not let him spend the night and I repeatedly told him that I just met him and I did not feel comfortable with him spending the night. So then he started asking when he could come over. I told him he could come over, but if he came over it would be for dinner at one of the restaurants in my building. He agreed and we discussed available dates. We finally got off the telephone around 2am!

The next day I did my general Google search of his name and where he went to college to make sure that he was who he said he was. I just wanted to verify that he went to the university that he said he attended, that he pledged Kappa as he said, and that the dates he attended undergrad coincided with the age that he told me he was. My general Google search verified that information.

Over the next few days we sent text messages and talked on the telephone. We were sending multiple text messages while I was waiting in line to get my driver's license. One of the messages Mr. Celibate sent me had to do with do I like oral sex and 69. I immediately called Mr. Celibate and told him that I don't discuss my sex life in detail via text message. I asked him if he was celibate, then why was he asking me about oral sex. Mr. Celibate told me that he was celibate, oral sex was allowed, and he had one of the best tongues in town! Oh No He Didn't!

Date night with Mr. Celibate finally arrived. I had a simple plan: I allowed him to come over, to buy me dinner, and to explore what would happen sexually. Based on the fact that more than half of his conversations were about sex I already knew that he was just interested in coming over for oral sex.

I went to the gym before he came over and I was just getting out of the shower when he called and said that he was on his way over. I was rushing to get myself put back together before he arrived at my building around 8pm. Because I was rushing I ended up just putting on a pair of shorts and a t-shirt so that I could go meet him when he arrived.

He bought us salad and pizza from the restaurant downstairs. After he got our dinner I brought him up to my place. We got the pizza and salad into the kitchen and then he got to check out my fabulous downtown Atlanta skyline view. As I was showing him around my bedroom the next thing I knew he was on his knees…Then, we went back to the kitchen area and ate our salad and pizza. After dinner we went back into my bedroom…and then we fell asleep.

After my date with Mr. Celibate I felt like Mr. Celibate was just too freaky for me to continue dating. I had to look in the dictionary to figure out if I had the wrong definition of celibate in my mind. I looked it up in the American Heritage Dictionary. It said celibate is one who abstains from sexual intercourse; sexual intercourse means coitus; and coitus means the physical union of male and female sexual organs, leading to orgasm and ejaculation of semen. After I looked up those definitions I was even more confused. After our date I was left wondering whether or not Mr. Celibate was still celibate or not.

Because I couldn't figure this one out I decided it would be best if I just stopped trying to figure it out and left Mr. Celibate alone. I still haven't figured it out. If anyone has figured it out, then please feel free to send me an email and let me know.

Advice for Men:

- Don't tell a woman that you are celibate and then tell her that you love to have oral sex as often as you can.

- Not every woman wants to get married and have kids with every man she meets, so if you just want to have a sexual relationship with a woman, then just tell her that up front. If she doesn't want the same type of relationship, then you can both move on quickly.

Advice for Women:

- When you are on a first date or during your first telephone conversation with a man and all he wants to talk about is sex/sex topics, then know that the only "relationship" that he wants to have with you is a sexual one.

- Know what type of relationship you want from the man before you have sex with him, you generally don't get to change it up once you have your game plan in place.

- Don't engage in detailed sexual communications with any man by text messaging.

OUTRAGEOUS DATING EXPERIENCE #6

Oh No He Didn't Make Me Think I Was On A Date With Chris Brown!

On Sunday November 8, 2009, I was going to the Atlanta Falcons versus the Washington Redskins game at the Georgia Dome. The weather was going to be warm that afternoon so my outfit for the game was a red Atlanta Falcons t-shirt (with a knot tied in the back so that I was showing off my sexy abs), my low rise black INC International Concepts pants, and my silver BCBGirls 4-inch high heel wedge sandals.

I got to the Georgia Dome before my girlfriend arrived and they were giving away eco-friendly reusable Atlanta Falcons bags. I didn't know if my girlfriend was going to get to the game before they ran out of bags so I was trying to get one for her and I noticed a nice looking guy coming into the Georgia Dome alone, no wedding band on, and with a Redskins jersey on. I figured that he would not want an Atlanta Falcons bag so I smiled at him and asked him if I could borrow his ticket so that I could get a bag for my girlfriend that was on her way to the game. Of course he said that I could borrow his ticket to get a second bag. Then we continued our conversation and exchanged telephone numbers so that we could continue communicating during (and after the game) via text messaging. I like to text during the Falcons games because it is too loud to talk on the phone during the game and the men that I meet at the Falcons games love when I text them during the game.

We exchanged several text messages during the first half of the game. Through our first-half texts I learned that he was single, he was in his thirties, he had no children, he worked as an engineer for an airline and as a sports referee, and he was interested in developing a relationship. I told him that I was single, had no children, was an attorney, and that I was also interested in a relationship. I also told him that I wasn't going to tell him my age. He tried to pry it out of me, but I wasn't in the mood to tell him so I just gave him various hilarious answers, including that I was 100 years old.

We met up at half-time, but I didn't end up on the 100 level with him (for reasons that I detail in Outrageous Dating Experience #15). We continued text messaging over the second half of the game as well. Later that evening we spoke on the telephone and continued getting to know one another. During the week we continued to talk and text.

By the end of the week we arranged to meet on Saturday, November 14, 2009 for our first date. We decided to go out to eat and then maybe to see a movie if it wasn't too late in the evening (I am an early bird and I don't do too well at movies that start after 9pm). We met at The Tavern restaurant at Phipps Plaza shopping mall in Atlanta. Over dinner we talked about his career path, my career path, his family, my family, and a good variety of other topics. The food was great and so was the conversation. After dinner we decided to walk around the mall and into a few of the clothing stores. We went into Armani Exchange, he tried on a few sweaters and I looked at a few items.

After we left Armani Exchange we were still having a good time laughing and joking. Then he asked me about my age and I finally told him that I would turn 40 the next weekend but I did not want to discuss it any further. Then he decided he wanted to act like he was in kindergarten and he started singing aloud that I was going to be 40 over and over again. I told him to stop but he kept on singing. So I turned away from him and started walking away. The next thing I knew he grabbed both of my back blue jean pockets, pulled me back towards him, and told me not to walk away from him. ("Mr. Physical"). Oh No He Didn't!

Mr. Physical pulled on my pockets so hard that I literally thought he was going to rip my pockets off of my jeans. I was highly concerned about Mr. Physical's actions for several reasons: first, I had never had this happen to me before; second, I couldn't remember what underwear I had on so if Mr. Physical ripped the pockets off my jeans I had no clue what I would be showing to everyone at the mall (either panties or my skin if I were wearing a thong or g-string); and third, I was going to be mad as hell if Mr. Physical had just ruined my new blue jeans because this was only the second time that I had worn them. There was a couple sitting on a mall bench in front of us and they looked as stunned as I was that Mr. Physical had grabbed me in this manner. I could tell that they wanted to ask me if I was okay. But I gave them a look that I had the situation with Mr. Physical under control.

After the "blue jean incident" with Mr. Physical I tried to act like everything was cool and we continued walking around the mall. We went into Ann Taylor and I looked at some clothes for work. We joked around about some of the items in the store and then we left the mall. After we left the mall Mr. Physical and I ended up at Atlantic Station for dessert. We ordered a slice of carrot cake to share while we watched a college football game. We talked to each other and we talked with the couple sitting next to us while we waited for the carrot cake to arrive. When the carrot cake arrived it was so huge that there was no way that the two of us could eat it all. After we finished eating the top layer of the cake I had the waiter wrap up the rest of it so that I could take it home and freeze it.

Then we left the restaurant and Mr. Physical walked me to my car. After Mr. Physical walked me to my car he picked me up so that he could give me a good night kiss. The good-night kiss was fine, but the way Mr. Physical picked me up to kiss me made me feel like I was a sack of potatoes or something. It was just an unpleasant feeling. I decided that I would discuss his physical ways and my discomfort with them the next time that I saw him.

Mr. Physical and I continued to talk and text regularly after our first date. We planned for Mr. Physical to come over to my place on Saturday night on his way back into town from a referee work trip, he would stay the night, and then he would take me to breakfast in the morning for my birthday.

On Saturday night Mr. Physical called when he was in the car on the highway traveling back to Atlanta to ask me if I wanted him to bring me anything. Of course I did. I told Mr. Physical that I wanted him to bring a mini-bottle four pack of Sutter Home wine. Mr. Physical stopped at the store and picked up the wine that I requested. Mr. Physical arrived at my place about an hour later.

After he got settled and I started drinking one of my mini-bottles of wine I decided it was time to discuss the blue jean incident with him. I told Mr. Physical that I did not appreciate the way that he grabbed my blue jean pockets when we were at the mall. Then I told him that I wasn't sure whether or not he even realized the amount of force that he used when he was pulling on my jeans was offensive. Mr. Physical said that he didn't mean to harm me in any way but he just didn't want me to walk away from him. I told him that I was not a sack of potatoes and he should not grab me in that manner in the future.

After our blue jean incident discussion we talked about other topics, we watched television, and then we fell asleep. Mr. Physical failed to tell me that he snored and was a wild sleeper. I ended up leaving to sleep in my second bedroom because I couldn't sleep in the same room with his loud ass snoring. While I was sleeping in the other bedroom I heard a loud noise, so I got up to find out what happened. I looked in the bedroom where Mr. Physical was sleeping and discovered that as Mr. Physical was sleeping he had moved the pillow so that everything on the nightstand was knocked onto the floor.

What a great way to start my 40th birthday. I returned to the bedroom where I was sleeping, said a quick prayer for morning to arrive fast, and then fell back asleep. Morning finally arrived and I was ready for a quick birthday breakfast with Mr. Physical. a bagel and coffee! I had some other celebrating to get to! (Outrageous Experience #15).

After my birthday date with Mr. Physical I decided to continue trying to develop a relationship with him. On Monday December 7th we started discussing plans for our next date, which was going to be on Friday, December 11th. On Wednesday we discussed our date plans again. He was joking that for the date I should wear a t-shirt that said I was sensitive. On Thursday Mr. Physical sent me a text message asking me what I wanted us to do/where did I want us to go on our date. I responded to Mr. Physical with a text message that included a list of suggestions. On Friday morning I sent him a text message asking him what time we were going out. Mr. Physical responded with a text message stating he didn't know what time we were going out. Oh No He Didn't! Then about four hours later he sent a text message that he was doing something with federal express. However, I had no clue what he was referring to. That was the last communication that I received from Mr. Physical on Friday before I turned off my cell phone at 10pm, right before I went to bed.

The next morning when I woke up I turned on my cell phone and there was a text message from Mr. Physical. I don't even remember what it said because I really wasn't interested. Mr. Physical sent at least four messages on Saturday and called at least two times. I ignored all of his Saturday calls and text messages, including the one that said you must really be mad.

Mr. Physical didn't text or call on Sunday. Then, on Monday, Mr. Physical sent a text message asking if he was out of the dog house yet. I finally decided that I would respond to Mr. Physical and told him that he put himself in the dog house. After that we exchanged text messages and spoke on the telephone. Mr. Physical claimed that his grandparent suffered a fractured bone Thursday evening and that was the reason that we didn't go out on Friday. If he really thought that I believed that story, then he is much dumber than I thought. Anyway, I let Mr. Physical believe that I believed his nonsensical story and we continued to communicate. I told Mr. Physical that he could make it up to me by taking me out the following Sunday.

All week we planned to go out on Sunday. We were going to go out to watch the NFL games at a sports bar and then have lunch. It was going to be a great afternoon, or so he thought. Sunday arrived and he sent me text messages and called me all day. I totally ignored him! I wasn't going anywhere with him. Mr. Physical was pissed! The next day I sent Mr. Physical a good morning text message. Mr. Physical sent me a text message asking what happened to me on Sunday. I told Mr. Physical that we were even now and we could arrange another date whenever we were both available.

Mr. Physical and I planned our next date for Christmas Eve. We were meeting at Lennox Mall after I got off work. I got off work at 11:30am and took the MARTA train to Lennox Mall. I was done with my Christmas gift shopping so I could enjoy browsing around the mall with Mr. Physical as he finished up his Christmas shopping. We met in Macy's near the ladies handbag section. Mr. Physical was planning to purchase a handbag for his mother for Christmas. After we finished in the handbag department and we were heading towards the Macy's mall entrance Mr. Physical wanted to discuss the fact that I stood him up on Sunday for our date. Now it would have been fine if he just wanted to discuss the matter. However, Mr. Physical grabbed me by my waist and pulled me towards him. I pulled Mr. Physical's hands off of me and told him that this was not appropriate and that I had told him not to put his hands on me in this manner before.

Then Mr. Physical grabbed me by my arms and pulled me towards him again. I again pulled his hands off of me and told him that this was not appropriate and to take his hands off of me. Lastly, he put his arm around my neck (he basically had me in a headlock but I was still standing) and pulled me towards him. Oh No He Didn't! I then pulled Mr. Physical's arm from around my neck and again told him to keep his hands off of me. Mr. Physical told me that my not going out with him on Sunday wasn't cool and that I shouldn't stand him up again. I told Mr. Physical whatever; just keep your hands off me. (Note: If Mr. Physical had literally hurt me, then I would have created the biggest fight scene possible in Macy's, we would have both been on the local news that evening, and he definitely would have been in jail for Christmas).

We continued walking into the mall. As we were walking to get lunch from Panera Mr. Physical began staring at me, like a two year old. I told Mr. Physical to stop staring at me. Mr. Physical told me that this was a free country and he could stare at me if he felt like it. I just ignored Mr.

Physical and kept walking toward the restaurant because I was starving and not in the mood for his silly games. Then Mr. Physical decided that he wanted to start walking into me purposely. Initially I thought that Mr. Physical was accidentally bumping into me and then I realized he was bumping into me on purpose. After I figured out that Mr. Physical was bumping into me on purpose I decided that I had had more than enough of Mr. Physical. I left Mr. Physical on Christmas Eve standing alone at Panera in Lennox Mall and I never looked back. I put him on Don't Answer Status before I even left the mall. After Mr. Physical was put on Don't Answer Status he called me two more times trying to get me to return to our date and then he sent me a text message that said I am giving you one last chance to come back. Oh No He Didn't!

Advice for Men:

- Don't try to use your physical strength to force a woman do what you want her to do.
- Treat women exactly how you want them to treat you… because payback is a bitch!

- If you stand a woman up for a date, then don't expect to get another date with her.

Advice for Women:

- If you are feeling physically threatened or intimidated by a man early on in your relationship, don't continue dating him because it is only going to get worse.
- If a man stands you up for a date, you have every right to stand him up for a date.
- If you are on a date and having a horrible time, then it is okay for you to leave the date when you can no longer tolerate his ass!

OUTRAGEOUS DATING EXPERIENCE #7

Oh No He Didn't Have An Online Dating Profile With A "Zillion" Misleading Photos!

In August 2005 I decided to give online dating a try. I created a profile on the website www.blackpeoplemeet.com. As soon as my profile was posted I received several messages from men interested in my profile. I read through the messages that I received and then reviewed their profiles before selecting the men that I was interested in responding to.

One of the men that I responded to had an online profile that included not one or two photos of himself, but at least 10 photographs of himself. ("Mr. Photoshop"). Mr. Photoshop's photos were from various activities, including from hanging out at home, at school, at his law school graduation, at the park, on vacation, and a few other activities. In Mr. Photoshop's photos he had on various outfits, from shorts to suits. Mr. Photoshop's online dating profile was a complete portfolio. Mr. Photoshop was single, had recently relocated to Atlanta from New Orleans due to Hurricane Katrina, was in his early thirties, no children, and was preparing to take the Georgia attorney examination.

After I read Mr. Photoshop's profile and viewed his photo album I responded to his message. Then we exchanged emails and then telephone numbers. My conversations with Mr. Photoshop weren't the best conversations I have ever had with a man, but I was willing to meet Mr. Photoshop for a first date. We decided to meet after work for a beverage at Starbucks.

When Mr. Photoshop arrived at Starbucks I recognized his face but not his body. Mr. Photoshop's body was nothing like the body he had in the zillion photographs posted on his online dating profile. Mr. Photoshop had gained at least 30 pounds since he had taken the pictures that were on his profile. Oh No He Didn't! I was speechless, yet I had to come up with some words to engage in a conversation with Mr. Photoshop.

OH NO HE DIDN'T!

I knew that I could not start the conversation off by telling him that I was highly disappointed that he felt the need to put an array of misleading slimmer pictures on his dating profile to lure me into meeting him. Therefore, I just pretended that I didn't notice that Mr. Photoshop had gained "a few extra pounds" since he had taken the photographs that were on his online profile. We ordered our beverages and then sat down for light conversation. The conversation with Mr. Photoshop was about the same as it was on the telephone, not the worst in the world and not the greatest. The best part about our date was that we were at Starbucks and I got to enjoy a cup of hot tea in the afternoon. I was so thrilled that I had planned to meet for a short date because I knew that I would have been completely miserable if I had been forced to endure a long dinner date with Mr. Photoshop. When I finished drinking my tea I told Mr. Photoshop that I had to get home to watch my favorite television show.

Mr. Photoshop left Starbucks in his car and I left in mine. Within five minutes of leaving Starbucks Mr. Photoshop called me on my cell phone to tell me that he had a great time. I responded to Mr. Photoshop as politely as I could that I had a nice time as well. I told him that I wanted to get off the phone to focus all of my attention on driving so that I could get home safely. After I got home I sent him an email that said it was a pleasure meeting him but I didn't feel that the chemistry was there. Instead of him either not responding any further or responding with a simple it was a pleasure meeting you as well, Mr. Photoshop sent me an email that said he didn't think the chemistry was there either but he still wanted to go out again because we could work on developing the chemistry later. I didn't even bother to reply to him and his name was replaced in my cell phone address book as Don't Answer.

I lived through my first actual internet date. It was a miracle that I actually went on this date because when I saw Mr. Photoshop in person and his body didn't look like any of the zillion photographs he had plastered all over his internet dating profile, I really wanted to drive right out of that Starbucks parking lot onto I-285 South, but I told myself that I could handle an hour long coffee date!

Advice for Men:

- Do not lie on your online dating profile by putting an entire photo album of photographs of you wearing clothes that you can no longer fit. In other words, if you have gained weight and can't wear any of the clothes that you are wearing in the pictures, then don't put any of those pictures on your dating profile.

- When a woman tells you that she would rather go home and watch television than have a second beverage with you, she is politely telling you that she is not interested in continuing the date.

- If a woman politely tells you that she is not interested in dating you, then accept it graciously and move onto meeting the next woman.

Advice for Women:

- When planning a first date with a man that you have met online, make sure that you plan an activity for a short time period so that if the date isn't going great then you don't have to be there too long. If the date is going good, then you have the option to stay longer.

- Make sure that a family member or a friend knows exactly when and where you are planning to meet for your internet date. Send that person a status update or two during your date so that they know you are safe.

- Also, provide your family member or friend with the man's cell phone number so that if you were to come up missing then they would quickly know where to start searching for you.

OUTRAGEOUS DATING EXPERIENCE #8

Oh No He Didn't Have An Online Dating Profile Listing Zero Kids, But He Had Three!

During my fall 2005 initial online dating experience I received a message from another man that appeared interesting. After I received his message I reviewed his profile. His profile said that he was single, no children, he was 5'11" tall, he was in his thirties, and he had recently moved to the Atlanta area. After I read his message and profile I responded back and we began communicating. We sent a few emails and then started talking on the telephone.

With online dating I prefer to exchange a maximum of three rounds of emails. If the email exchange is going okay, then I exchange cell phone numbers to talk by telephone. I know within the first or second telephone conversation if I want to meet a man in person or not. If I am interested in meeting him in person, then we generally meet within two weeks for a first date. I am not the type that enjoys purely an e-relationship where we just email back and forth for months on end.

During our second conversation on the telephone he started talking about his children. I was sitting on the telephone looking extremely perplexed. I said to myself either the picture on his profile was extremely gorgeous and I overlooked the fact that he had children or I must have misread his profile because I don't remember reading that he had children. Immediately after we got off the telephone I went on the internet and pulled up his profile. ("Mr. Childless"). His profile was exactly as I had remembered; it stated that he didn't have children.

The next evening we were talking on the telephone while I was at the grocery store. I am not sure what we were talking about but I decided to question Mr. Childless about his online profile. I asked Mr. Childless if I could ask him a question...and of course he took the bait. Mr. Childless said of course you can ask me a question. I asked him why did you lie on your profile and list that you didn't have any children. Mr. Childless said "I never lied on my internet profile." I don't have any little kids. My children are teenagers and young adults and when you list the information on the internet dating sites they are asking about little kids and I don't have any little kids. Oh No He Didn't! For those of you that weren't on blackpeoplemeet.com in the fall of 2005, the question they listed regarding children didn't ask you to check the box if your children were under the age of 13; it had a simple click "yes" box if you had children and a click "no" box if you didn't have children.

Mr. Childless decided that because his children were over the age of 13, that he didn't have children and he should click the no children answer box on his internet dating profile. That night I wanted to call my mother and tell her that I guess I was no longer her daughter because I was over the age of 13. Based on Mr. Childless's theory, everyone reading this book over the age of 13 is no longer their parent's child and if you have children over the age of 13 then you should not include them on your online dating profile because you no longer have them.

Despite the fact that Mr. Childless lied on his profile about having children, I still agreed to go on a first date with him. Plus, I really wanted to find out what else he may have lied about on his profile by meeting him in person. I already knew at this point that Mr. Childless would not become someone that I would seriously date, but he could possibly become a friend that I could socialize with.

Mr. Childless and I agreed to go to the movies for our first date. I chose the movies because I knew that I would enjoy the date because I really wanted to see some of the movies that were playing at the time. When I saw Mr. Childless walking into the movie theatre I immediately knew that Mr. Childless had lied about another item on his online profile. I am 5' 10" tall barefoot. I can tell a man's height from a distance and it is one of the important items I look for when I am reading a man's online dating profile because I hate dating men that are shorter than I am.

As I mentioned previously, Mr. Childless listed that he was 5'11" tall on his profile, so I made sure that I wore my athletic shoes on the date in an effort to remain as close to 5'10" tall as possible. When Mr. Childless walked up to me to officially introduce himself the top of his head was barely at the bottom of my chin. So there was no way on this earth that he was 5'11" and I knew if I had asked him why he lied on his profile about his height he would have told me that he was 5'11" and that he never lied on his profile.

Because he lied about not having children on his online dating profile, it didn't surprise me that he wasn't as tall as he said he was in person. Despite this second (and major lie in my book) I stayed and enjoyed the movie. I believe we spoke once or twice after the date. However, when he lied about having children, then said he never lied about it, and then lied about his height, I just didn't have the desire to continue getting to know him any further.

Advice for Men:

- If you have children (no matter how old they are), then check the box that says yes for the question regarding do you have children on the online dating profile questionnaire.

- List the ages of your children in your profile so that someone viewing your profile will have the information they need to decide if they want to date you with the children that you have.

- If you actually plan on meeting the women that you are communicating with from internet dating websites, then don't lie on your profile about your height by more than one inch.

Advice for Women:

- Make sure you have a set of internet dating "rules" that you follow such as: how many emails you want to exchange with a man before giving him your cell phone number; how long you want to communicate with a man before you have a first date; what lies from his profile are you willing to accept/what lies are deal breakers; and a list of your favorite public places where you are willing to go for your first date.

- If a man has lies on his online dating profile, don't be afraid to ask him about it. If you don't like his response, don't be afraid to move on to the next man!

OUTRAGEOUS DATING EXPERIENCE #9

Oh No He Didn't Tell Me He Was An Attorney But He Wasn't!

Summer 2006 I decided it was time for another attempt at online dating. I put my profile back on www.blackpeoplemeet.com. A man responded to my profile and sent me an initial communication. I reviewed his profile and responded back to his communication. His profile stated that he was a single attorney in the Atlanta area. ("Mr. Esquire"). We exchanged a few emails through blackpeoplemeet.com and then started talking on the telephone. We discussed meeting in person for gelato (Italian ice cream), but we never actually finalized a plan for meeting. After our initial plans to meet never materialized we didn't email or talk for a few months.

However, in November 2006 Mr. Esquire called me and we started talking again. We discussed our failed plans to meet for gelato back in the summer and then decided that since it was fall and too cold for gelato we would meet for hot chocolate. Mr. Esquire suggested that we could meet at a coffee shop in Atlantic Station because it was near the law firm where he worked. I asked Mr. Esquire which law firm he worked at. Mr. Esquire told me he worked at one of the large law firms in Atlanta with the initials "K&S." I told Mr. Esquire that one of my best friends in Atlanta was also an attorney at that law firm.

Mr. Esquire and I met for drinks at the coffee shop in Atlantic Station. The hot chocolate was decent. The conversation was decent. After the date, I concluded that it was an average date; it wasn't the best first date I had ever had and it wasn't the worst first date I had ever had. While I was in the car on the way back to my office I sent a text message to my girlfriend that worked at K&S to ask her if she knew Mr. Esquire and to tell her that I had just gone on a date with him. She sent me a text back that said she didn't know him and there was no one that worked at her law firm with that name.

I immediately sent Mr. Esquire a text message letting him know that my girlfriend that was an attorney at K&S told me that he didn't work there. Mr. Esquire responded to me that he worked at K&S as a contract attorney. So, I then sent a text to my girlfriend and asked her to check and see if Mr. Esquire was working at K&S as a contract attorney. My girlfriend checked and responded back to me that he was not working at K&S in any capacity. I sent Mr. Esquire another text letting him know that I knew he was not working at K&S in any capacity and that I did not believe that he was an attorney.

When I got back to my office I went on the State Bar of Georgia's website and typed in Mr. Esquire's name on the Member Directory search page. The search results were no member attorney found by that name. I sent Mr. Esquire a text message that he was not listed as an attorney on the State Bar of Georgia's website. Mr. Esquire responded to me that he had elected not to be listed as a member on the State Bar of Georgia's Member Directory website. Mr. Esquire had done his research because attorney members of the State Bar of Georgia have the right to be excluded from the State Bar of Georgia's internet member directory.

However, I called the State Bar of Georgia to ask for a verification of whether Mr. Esquire was an attorney in Georgia. They confirmed that he was not an attorney in Georgia. I sent Mr. Esquire a text message that I had confirmed with the State Bar of Georgia that he was not an attorney in Georgia. So his next lie was that he had taken the attorney bar examination in Georgia and he was waiting for the test results and he was a licensed attorney in New York. Oh No He Didn't! Both of these statements were lies and I told him that I knew he was lying.

The attorney licensing examination is given across the United States two times per year: at the end of February with the results released by the end of May and at the end of July with the results released by the end of October. Generally (and specifically in Georgia), no one is waiting for examination results in November. I also checked on the attorney directory for attorneys licensed in New York and Mr. Esquire was not listed.

Mr. Esquire really wanted to keep playing the lying game even though he had been fully busted. I imagine that I was the first woman that had figured out that Mr. Esquire was not an attorney and he just didn't want to accept the fact that I wasn't going to play into his game. I was shocked that a man would lie to an attorney that he was an attorney! I was shocked that Mr. Esquire would think that he could get away with lying to me. I was shocked that Mr. Esquire would think that he could get away with lying to me that he worked at K&S when I told him that one of my best friends in Atlanta was an attorney at the law firm he claimed he worked at. Did he think I wasn't going to ask her if she knew him? There are not that many African American attorneys working at the large law firms, so all of the minority attorneys at least know of their fellow minority attorney coworkers.

You already know that Mr. Esquire was put on Don't Answer Status. But he kept sending me text messages. Mr. Esquire even sent me a text message with a picture of the city he was supposedly flying over on his way to a legal assignment. I ignored him and deleted the text.

I just hope and pray that Mr. Esquire has stopped pretending that he is an attorney! And I really hope and pray that he hasn't married some woman that he met on the internet and she thinks that her husband is an attorney and he isn't!

Advice for Men:

- Don't lie about your profession, especially when it is a licensed profession that can be easily verified.
- If a woman that you have only dated once catches you in a major lie, then just give up on dating her. Don't keep telling more lies in an effort to try and continue dating her.

Advice for Women:

- When a man tells you that he is a lawyer, doctor, or any other profession that requires a license by the State, go on the internet and verify that he is in fact licensed before you go on your first date with him.
- If you can't verify that the man is the licensed professional that he told you he is, then don't be afraid to ask him about the fact that you can't verify his license. If he is lying about his occupation, then he is also lying about other issues.
- When a man tells you that he works with or went to school with your friend (or acquaintance), then make

sure you check with your friend to verify that he is telling you the truth. You can never be too careful.

OUTRAGEOUS DATING EXPERIENCE #10

Oh No He Didn't Tell Me "I Said To Myself Let Me Call This Knucklehead & See What She's Doing!"

During my fall 2005 online dating experience I had another outrageous experience. I received a message from a man that was interested in me about a week or two before Christmas. I reviewed the message he sent me and then I reviewed his profile. He was single, no children, in his thirties, a dentist, and lived in the metropolitan Atlanta area. I reviewed his photos and he looked nice. I sent him a message that I was interested in getting to know him. Then we exchanged a few emails and then we exchanged telephone numbers.

Wc had some decent telephone conversations and setup our first date. We decided to meet at the Outback Steakhouse closest to my house for dinner on December 23, 2005. I remember the date because it was right before Christmas. Prior to meeting for our first date I did verify on Georgia's Secretary of State Professional Licensing Website - License Verification page that he was in fact a licensed dentist. If you have any questions about why I verified his dental license, then (re)read Outrageous Dating Experience #9.

He was prompt for our date, he looked exactly like his photographs from his online dating profile, and he was actually the height that he listed on his online dating profile. The first five minutes of this internet date were going better than all of my prior internet dates combined. We had a nice dinner and good conversation. Later that evening after we left the restaurant we spoke on the telephone. I invited him to join my family and me for Christmas dinner because he was going to be alone for Christmas... he wasn't planning to travel to home for the holidays, his family wasn't traveling to Atlanta, and no one in the area had invited him over for Christmas dinner. ("Mr. Personality").

I extended the dinner invitation to Mr. Personality because I love sharing the Christmas holidays with family and friends, not because I was trying to rush into a relationship with Mr. Personality or that I was just dying for him to meet my mom and my sisters. I explained this to Mr. Personality and told him that I would not be offended if he declined the invitation. I also told Mr. Personality that if he preferred, he could come over for holiday leftovers after my family left town on December 27th. Mr. Personality chose the December 27th dinner option.

On Christmas Day Mr. Personality called to wish me a Merry Christmas. I told Mr. Personality about all of the gifts that I had exchanged with my mom and my sisters. Then I asked Mr. Personality what he had received from his family. Mr. Personality said he that didn't get any gifts. Mr. Personality said that his parents had sent him a gift but it hadn't arrived yet. I felt so bad for Mr. Personality because I loved exchanging Christmas gifts and I had just received a ton of fabulous gifts that I loved.

I changed the subject and asked Mr. Personality what his plans were for the day. Mr. Personality told me that he was planning to watch the NBA games with a group of neighbors. Mr. Personality had to watch the game with his neighbors because he didn't have cable at his apartment. Mr. Personality said he didn't like the company that provided cable service to his complex so he wasn't going to pay for cable service. I told Mr. Personality that my Christmas day afternoon would be spent cooking the rest of our family holiday dinner, eating dinner, and then watching the NBA games with my sisters.

We had several conversations later that afternoon and into the evening. Mr. Personality called me back that night upset because he had to try to and watch the NBA games on his computer (Note: this was 2005 and watching NBA games on the internet wasn't as easy as it is in 2010) because his neighbors were smoking weed while watching the game he left the gathering because he didn't like the atmosphere. I felt so bad for Mr. Personality because he was having a horrible Christmas and I was having the best Christmas ever with my family. Mr. Personality could have been watching the game with us, but he let his male ego get in the way of having fun.

The day after Christmas I got up early and headed to the stores for the after Christmas sales. While I was out shopping I made sure that I bought a few small things for Mr. Personality to try to cheer up his Christmas season. I got Mr. Personality a Christmas card, another small gift that I don't recall, but it was less than $10 on sale. I also bought a baking pan and the ingredients to make homemade brownies from scratch, because he mentioned that he really liked brownies. I decided I would make the brownies for the holiday leftover meal desert.

Later that day I asked Mr. Personality if he received the Christmas gifts from his parents. Mr. Personality replied that he received his gift and it was cash. I asked Mr. Personality what he was going to buy with the cash and he said he was just going to put it in the bank. I thought to myself that was really boring because he hadn't gotten any gifts from anyone and then he finally gets a gift which is really a gift to go out and get his own gift and he simply decides to put the entire gift in the bank. He could have at least put half of it in the bank and then spent the other half of it on a gift for himself, especially since there were some fabulous after Christmas sales in 2005!

December 27th finally arrived. I drove my family back to the airport, cleaned up the house, and then started getting the house ready for my date with Mr. Personality. I gathered the ingredients together to make the brownies and started reading the recipe. I hadn't made brownies from scratch in years, so the only part of the recipe that "surprised" me was that I had to sift the flour twice. After I got the flour sifted the rest of the recipe was easy and the brownies I baked were perfect. It took less than an hour to make the brownies, and it wasn't a major undertaking because December is my favorite time of year for baking! It's an annual tradition of mine to bake cookies and cakes for holiday gift giving.

Mr. Personality arrived at my house on time for our second date. We ate dinner and then I gave him the Christmas card, the small gift, and the fresh from the oven home baked brownies. Mr. Personality was thrilled. Mr. Personality thanked me over and over again for everything. I told Mr. Personality that I was happy to share my Christmas holiday with him.

After we were done eating we were sitting in the family room having a conversation while the television was on. The conversation wasn't continuously flowing, so I was trying my best to keep the conversation going. As I was asking Mr. Personality a question he interrupted and said it sounds like you like to talk a lot! Oh No He Didn't!

Since he thought I was talking too much I decided I wasn't going to say anything else to him. Then I turned away from him and started watching television. Mr. Personality tried to engage me in conversation and I just looked at him with a blank stare and remained silent. After about fifteen minutes of my silence Mr. Personality decided that he was going to leave.

I told Mr. Personality that I was packing up the brownies and the brownie pan for him because I would never be making brownies for him again. Mr. Personality thought that I was joking, but I was as serious as a heart attack about never making him brownies again. (Note: I haven't made brownies for him or for anyone else since December 27, 2005.) Mr. Personality left and took the brownies in the brownie pan with him. However, Mr. Personality wasn't gone long. Mr. Personality came back about ten minutes later and apologized. I accepted Mr. Personality's apology and invited him back in. I decided that he had been given the silent treatment long enough and it was time to resume our conversation. However, I told him that I was never changing my mind about the brownies.

Mr. Personality and his mother were very close. So Mr. Personality decided that he needed to tell his mother all of the details of our date, including the fact that I told him that I would never make him brownies again. Mr. Personality's mother told him to give me a message…she said: Don't worry about it baby, I will make you brownies and you don't have to worry about her making you brownies ever again. I told Mr. Personality to thank his mother for me because now he was definitely never getting any more brownies from me again.

After the "brownie incident" we decided to spend New Year's Eve ("NYE") together. Both of us agreed that we didn't want to spend the evening out at a big party or to risk being out on the road with potential drunk drivers at midnight, so we decided to spend the evening at my place. Mr. Personality didn't drink alcoholic beverages, so I purchased a bottle of Asti Spumante Champagne for myself to drink during our home NYE celebration. I also purchased a bag of Tostitos tortilla chips and salsa for us to share. (I normally only eat Tostitos on NYE, Super bowl Sunday,

Memorial Day and the 4th of July because that's when I have company over to share the large size bag and Frito Lay doesn't sell Tostitos in small serving size bags.)

Mr. Personality arrived at my house for our NYE celebration around 9pm. We decided to start the evening off by watching a movie. As we were watching the movie I ate some Tostitos and salsa. After the movie was over we turned on the NYE television shows to watch the countdown to 2006. I sipped on champagne as we watched the countdown into the New Year. I had 3 champagne flutes full of champagne, which is the amount that I had intended to drink when I purchased the bottle of champagne. However, I guess my food and alcoholic beverage consumption was offensive to Mr. Personality because after midnight he told me that he had been counting the number of tortilla chips that I had eaten and the number of glasses of champagne that I had drank. Oh No He Didn't!

Now, if I was overweight and I had consumed the entire bag of tortilla chips, then I would have understood Mr. Personality's oversight and commentary on my food intake; however, his actions were totally absurd and unnecessary. If I had been the designated driver and then consuming champagne, then I would have understood Mr. Personality's concern regarding the 3 glasses of champagne that I had consumed. Or if I had been exhibiting any prior signs of being an alcoholic, then it would have been more than appropriate for Mr. Personality to have been concerned about my alcoholic beverage consumption. However, none of this was the case. Our NYE date came to an end shortly after Mr. Personality told me he had been counting my food and drink intake!

Despite the wonderful start to 2006 with Mr. Personality, I continued talking with him. Mr. Personality would call every week to tell me that I could invite him over to watch the NFL football playoff games. Mr. Personality would make these requests repeatedly because he didn't have cable at his apartment and he really wanted to watch the NFL football games on my high definition television with DIRECTV™. However, I rarely invited him over to watch the games because I felt that he should have used his own money to pay for his own cable or satellite television to watch the NFL football games at his place.

One weekend I decided I wasn't going to answer Mr. Personality's calls because I knew he was just going to say

that I could invite him over to watch the playoff games.
Several days later Mr. Personality called and I decided I
would take his call. I answered the phone and Mr.
Personality told me: "I said to myself let me call this
knucklehead and see what she's doing." Oh No He Didn't!
just call me up on my telephone that I pay the bill for and
call me a knucklehead!

Google's internet definition of a knucklehead is a
stupid person! Wordnetweb.princeton.edu/perl.webwn says
a knucklehead is used to express a low opinion of someone's
intelligence! I have a Bachelor's Degree in Accounting Cum
Laude with Business Departmental Honors from Kentucky
State University; I have a Law Degree and a Masters of
Business of Administration Degree from Duke University
that I completed in 3.5 years (and I am the first student at
Duke to have ever done so); I am a Georgia Certified Public
Accountant and an Attorney… and Mr. Personality is calling
me a knucklehead. Oh No He Didn't!

The knucklehead comment was the last straw. Mr.
Personality was a nice person but I could no longer deal with
his lack of social and dating skills. He was simply deleted
from my phone.

Advice for Men:

- When a woman is trying to keep the getting to know you conversation going, don't insult her by telling her it seems like she likes to talk a lot.

- When you are celebrating New Year's Eve with your date, don't tell her that you are counting how many glasses of champagne she is having and how much food she is eating.

- Don't tell the woman you are dating that she is a knucklehead. In the event that you feel that she is a knucklehead and you want to tell someone that you feel this way, then tell it to everyone else in the world but her!

Advice for Women:

- The legal definition of a "Reasonable Man" is "[A] person whose notions and standards of behavior and responsibility correspond with those generally obtained among ordinary people in our society at the present time…" R.F.V. Heuston, *Salmond On The Law of Torts* 56 (17th ed. 1977).

- o It is okay to stop dating a nice man when he totally lacks a reasonable man standard level of dating skills.
- o A man that calls you up and tells you that you are a knucklehead lacks a reasonable man standard level of dating skills!
- The relationship that a man has with his mother when you start dating him won't change based on the length of time that you date him. It is what it is, no matter how much you may want it to change it won't! Accept it as it is, or find someone else to date.

OUTRAGEOUS DATING EXPERIENCE #11

Oh No He Didn't Ask Me "Can I Ask You A Personal Question...Do You Have Any Panties On Under Your Dress?"

In the spring of 2008 I decided that I would give online dating another try. This time I decided that I would try www.match.com. I posted a new online profile with updated pictures. After I posted my profile I performed a search of men based on certain criteria and then browsed through the results. I sent a few "flirt" messages to the men that were of interest. I also received several messages from men that were interested in communicating with me. When I received these messages I reviewed their profile photographs.

If I didn't like the man's photograph, then I would send him a quick "thanks, but no thanks" reply and then delete his message. If there was no photograph on his profile, then I would send him a request to send me a photograph. If he responded to me with a photograph and I wasn't thrilled with his looks, then I just didn't respond back to his email. While I can't speak for all women, I can speak for myself and I am just as visual as men are and if I am not physically attracted to a man then I can't date him.

One of the men that I connected with on www.match.com I was physically attracted to, so I decided to review his profile (while hoping that his photos were accurate). He was single (and never married), in his late thirties, had a son that was a freshman in college, had completed his undergraduate education at a historically black college, was currently enrolled in a Masters of Business Administration ("MBA") degree program at a local university, worked for a local utility company as an electrical engineer, and he owned his own company that he operated part-time. From reviewing his profile we had a lot in common: the same marital status, we both attended a historically black college for undergrad, I already had a

MBA, I had worked for a utility company when I completed my MBA, and I was self-employed. Based on all that we had in common, I decided to send him a reply message that I was interested in communicating with him. ("Mr. Match"). We exchanged a few emails. Mr. Match sent me an email asking me the dumbest online dating question there is: why are you on match.com? I have always operated under the theory of if you ask me a dumb ass question, then I am going to give you a dumb ass answer. Therefore, I told Mr. Match that I was on match.com because I was psychic and knew that I had to get on there because I knew that he was going to start communicating with me and how else was I going to meet him. Mr. Match didn't appreciate my answer. What else was I supposed to say? I was on match.com for the same reason Mr. Match was on there…to meet new people to date. After that Mr. Match began asking more intelligent questions and we exchanged telephone numbers.

We had several telephone conversations. I enjoyed talking with Mr. Match, despite his thick southern accent. After several conversations, I verified that he was actually enrolled in the MBA program by going on the university's website and checking for his name in the student directory. I also verified his electrical license with the Georgia Secretary of State on the license verification website.

Next, Mr. Match and I arranged to meet for our first date, a Saturday night dinner date around 10pm. Note: I admit that I am one of the pickiest eaters on the planet (my family and friends would say that this is an understatement); however, I decided that I would let him pick the restaurant because he expressed an interest in wanting to do so. Additionally, I didn't mind allowing Mr. Match to pick the restaurant because I had planned to eat dinner before I met him at the restaurant so that if the food wasn't good then my mood for the rest of the date wouldn't be negatively impacted by hunger. I can be a bitch when I'm starving (some people that know me well would also say this is an understatement). Mr. Match picked a restaurant that wasn't too far from where I lived, but I had never heard of it before and I wasn't familiar with where it was located. I told Mr. Match I was fine going to the restaurant as long as my car's navigation system could locate it and guide me to it.

After we got off the phone I showered, put on my clothes, put on my makeup, got my hair together, and got my accessories together for our dinner date. Then I proceeded to my car, turned the car on, then called Mr. Match so that I could put the restaurant location information into the car navigation system to guide me to the restaurant. Mr. Match didn't answer. I figured that he was probably still in the midst of getting ready for our date so I waited another five minutes and then called Mr. Match back. Mr. Match didn't answer. I sent Mr. Match a text message. He didn't respond. I waited another five minutes and then called Mr. Match again. Mr. Match didn't answer. I turned my car off, went back inside my building and then back inside my condo. I left my cell phone on and made myself available to speak to Mr. Match or receive text messages from him for an additional fifteen minutes. After the fifteen minute period expired I turned my cell phone off for the night.

After I turned off the cell phone that Mr. Match had the number to, I turned on my second cell phone line so that I could call my sister to tell her about being stood up by Mr. Match. My sister and I joked and laughed about what excuses Mr. Match was going to have for standing me up. After talking with my sister I decided that I would at least listen to the excuses that Mr. Match inevitably would come up with for standing me up and then I would decide whether or not I would even bother giving him another chance for a first date.

Sunday morning I turned my cell phone on and I had several voice messages and text messages from Mr. Match. Mr. Match said that he could explain what happened and to please give him a call so that he could explain. I knew that I was going to call Mr. Match to hear this fabulous explanation; however, I wasn't going to call him any time soon. I had other social plans for my Sunday.

I went to see Sex In The City at the movies with my girlfriend and then we went out to eat a late lunch and drink cosmopolitans at Arizona's restaurant near Stonecrest Mall. I told her about being stood up the night before and about all of the text messages and voice messages that I received from Mr. Match that morning. We got a good laugh about it. We then decided that we wanted to hear his reason(s) for standing me up during our lunch so that we could get some more laughs about it.

I called Mr. Match and put him on speaker phone. Mr. Match told me that one of his employees called him after we got off the phone said he desperately needed to get paid immediately, so Mr. Match had to go take the employee his pay and because he was in such a rush to take his employee the money he accidentally forgot his cell phone at home so he wasn't able to call me, answer my calls, or respond to my text messages. My girlfriend and I laughed so hard it was extremely difficult for me to keep my composure while I was on the phone with Mr. Match. However, I managed to sound sympathetic and to tell Mr. Match that I fully understood the demands of being an employer and having to deal with emergency employee issues.

I told Mr. Match that we were cool and we would just plan another first date and that I would be selecting the date, time, and location, since Mr. Match had the first opportunity and he blew it. I was extremely reluctant to give Mr. Match a second chance, however, I decided that I would keep my word and allow Mr. Match a second chance to try and make another first impression. I told Mr. Match he was fighting an uphill battle, but I was willing to try.

During the next week we were in communication daily, by telephone and by text. By the end of the week I had forgiven Mr. Match for standing me up for our first date, but I certainly hadn't forgotten. I was finally ready to resume discussing our "first" date plans again. We decided that we would go out to dinner on Sunday and I decided that we would meet at the Cheesecake Factory at the Cumberland Mall because I enjoyed the food there and I needed to get some items from Macy's. Additionally, if Mr. Match stood me up for our date, then I could still enjoy my evening by taking myself to dinner after a quick bit of shopping at the mall.

Mr. Match actually arrived for our date. Mr. Match was cuter than the photos on his online profile and he was actually the height he listed on his profile. The conversation went well. We even briefly discussed our failed original first date and Mr. Match apologized again for standing me up. I told him that I wasn't one that was good at giving second chances, but I allowed myself to make an exception for him. After dinner we stood outside and continued our conversation. Then we hugged and the date ended.

Over the next several weeks we continued communicating and had at least one more date. However, we both had very busy schedules. Mr. Match was working full-time and part-time while taking MBA courses. I was working full-time while trying to sell my former rental house in Austell, Georgia. One afternoon in late June while Mr.

Match was on a business trip in Helen, Georgia and I was working at my former rental house we were on the phone joking around and I mentioned driving up to Helen to meet him for dinner and to help him with his MBA homework in his hotel room. Our joke turned into a date for that evening.

After I finished working at my former rental house I headed home to get ready for our date. Helen, Georgia is 90 miles north of Atlanta, but it takes almost two hours to get up there because half of the trip is on two-lane roads thru the mountains. Therefore, I wanted to get on the road as soon as I could so that I would get up there before dark. I showered and then took what seemed like forever trying to select the perfect date outfit. I decided to wear one of my favorite summer dresses, which was a simple white sleeveless cotton dress with a scoop neck. After I put the white dress on I debated about wearing it because I was already wearing one of my favorite matching bra and panty sets that had a light green pattern on it and I was wondering if it was going to be visible through the white dress. Finally, I decided I wasn't going to waste any more time debating on what to wear because I was wasting daylight driving time; I was just going to keep on everything that I already had on and I wasn't going to worry about whether or not someone could see my green bra and panty set on through my dress. Then I gathered the rest of the items I needed for the overnight trip and got on the road.

The drive to Helen wasn't bad. I enjoy driving and going to new places. When I arrived in Helen I met Mr. Match at the hotel and then we drove to a local restaurant for dinner. Initially Mr. Match wanted to sit at an outdoor table. As we were about to sit at the outdoor table I told him that I would need to get my jacket from the trunk of my car if we were going to sit outside because it was chilly and Mr. Match said well that's because you're naked. Oh No He Didn't! just say I was naked. (See page 135 for a picture of me in the "Naked Dress").

I really wanted to clown and act a fool at this point; however, I had taken my time to get nicely dressed for this date and then I had just driven ninety minutes to get to this date so I was going to remain calm and ignore Mr. Match's ignorant statement.

Mr. Match then said that we could just sit at an indoor table. Mr. Match and I sat at the indoor table and ordered our dinner. We had a nice conversation. We talked about the training course that he had been attending in Helen. Mr. Match told me about the rounds of golf he had played while he had been in Helen and he introduced me to some of the people that he knew in the restaurant. Then, Mr. Match says: "Can I ask you a personal question?" I said Oh Lord, sure what is it? Mr. Match said: "Are you wearing any panties under your dress because I can't tell?" Oh No He Didn't! just ask me if I was wearing panties.

Why in the world would Mr. Match decide that this was an appropriate question to ask me, and especially at dinner? As my sister asked me, what was he going to do or say if I had told him no, I am not wearing any panties? As my mom said years ago, I am not aware of any laws requiring women to wear panties. Anyway, I told Mr. Match yes, I am wearing panties and a matching bra. Then Mr. Match told me I know you are wearing a bra because I can see it through your dress. I should have immediately left his ass in the restaurant at that point, but I didn't.

We finished our dinner and conversation. Then we returned to his hotel room. When we got to his hotel room Mr. Match asked me what time I was leaving in the morning. I told Mr. Match that I would be leaving around 6am because

I had to get back for a court hearing later in the morning. Mr. Match said great because that way I would be gone before any of his coworkers would see me leaving in the morning. Oh No He Didn't! Once again I disregarded Mr. Match's ignorant statement so that we could continue our date. Then Mr. Match told me to keep my voice down because he didn't want his coworkers that were in the rooms nearby to hear my voice in his room. Oh No He Didn't! I thought to myself am I in a dream and are we in high school, sneaking into his bedroom to spend the night and his parents may catch us … did I miss something?

I brought myself back into reality and instead of cussing Mr. Match out I told Mr. Match it was time for him to make me an apple martini. In case you were wondering, Mr. Match already had the ingredients for my favorite drink in the room because I asked him to get the Belvedere vodka and apple pucker before I arrived in town.

As I was sipping my apple martini, and my nerves had calmed down, I told Mr. Match to take out his MBA assignment for me to review. I continued sipping my apple martini while reading through his textbook, syllabus, assignment sheet, and class notes. I was trying to take myself back to the days of doing statistics homework at Duke so that I could help Mr. Match complete his homework. However, my statistics memory wasn't working too well and I wasn't much help. After about 45 minutes of trying to figure it out, we both decided that MBA homework time was over.

Then it was lights out. Mr. Match went to sleep in one bed and left me lying in the other bed. No hug, no kiss, no nothing. So I decided that I would go get in the bed that he was in and at least try to snuggle up next to him. However, that effort pretty much failed. He was on one side of the bed and I was on the other side of the bed. What the hell! It was around 12:30am. I finally decided that I had had enough of Mr. Match for the evening. I decided at that moment that I was going home because if I was going to sleep in the bed alone or if I was going to sleep in the bed with zero affection, then I could sleep at home alone in my own bed. Plus, I definitely didn't need to drive home from Helen in the morning with the rush hour traffic trying to make it to court on time. Thank God for my navigation system and my cell phone. I used both of them for almost the entire drive home. I made it home by 2am.

The next morning I received a text message from Mr. Match which said that I was wild for leaving at 12:30am. Whatever! The funny thing is that I wasn't mad at him; I just wasn't in the mood for Sleepless in Helen!

A few months later the communications between Mr. Match and I resumed. Mr. Match advised me that he had successfully completed his statistics class and he received a good grade. Mr. Match went on to tell me that he was taking a managerial accounting class and he needed a tutor. I told Mr. Match that I was a much better tutor for managerial accounting than I was for statistics. Mr. Match already knew that I was a Certified Public Accountant ("CPA") and then I told him that I tested out of the managerial accounting class for my MBA program at Duke so I could provide him with help if he needed it.

Mr. Match called to schedule his first accounting tutorial session at my place. The session went well. I reviewed his assignment, class notes, and textbook. This time around I assisted him with his project and provided him with the proper questions that he should ask his professor to complete the assignment. It was a miracle that we spent a few hours together and he didn't do or say anything stupid or insulting.

The next accounting "tutorial session" didn't go as well. On the phone Mr. Match claimed that he needed help with his take home final exam. However, when Mr. Match arrived he handed me his final exam for me to work on the problems and then stretched out on my couch, grabbed my remote control, changed the station, and then started watching television. Mr. Match actually thought that he was going to watch my television while I was going to complete his take home final exam for him and then he had the nerve to get an attitude when I told him that he totally had it wrong. Oh No He Didn't!

This was the day that Mr. Match was finally going to hear what was really on my mind. I told Mr. Match that I already had a Bachelors Degree in Accounting with Business Departmental Honors, I had a CPA, and a Masters of Business Administration so there was absolutely no need for me to ever complete another accounting examination again in my life. If he seriously thought I was going to complete his final exam for him he had completely lost his mind. Then I yelled at him to pack his school shit up and get the hell out because it was time for him to go. I escorted Mr. Match out of my place and then out of the building and I haven't seen or heard from him since. You already know that Mr. Match was placed on Don't Answer Status that night!

Advice for Men:

- When you don't like your date's outfit you have several options, none of which should include telling her that she is naked.
  - Option 1: You can choose to say nothing about her outfit, continue with the date and then never see her again.
  - Option 2: You can choose to say nothing about her outfit but offer her your coat or jacket for her to wear so that it will cover up her outfit.
  - Option 3: You can find a favorable way to discuss her outfit, such as complimenting her on the color of her outfit or her shoes or anything that you can find that you like about her outfit. Once the two of you start discussing her outfit, then you can find out if she either loves her outfit and always

dresses in this manner or if she hates her outfit and would not dress in this manner in the future. Keep in mind that one day you are probably going to wear an outfit that she hates and she isn't going to tell you that you look like a hot mess!

- If are dating a woman and you are not in a sexually intimate relationship with her, then DO NOT ask her if she is wearing panties. No matter how bad you want to know the answer to that question, do not ask her! That is not an appropriate date question.

- Don't ask a woman that you are dating to do your school homework or exams for you because you could find yourself expelled from school for academic misconduct if she reports your unethical behavior to the school.

Advice for Women:

- Don't slap your date if he tells you that you're naked because your outfit is too skimpy. You don't want to get arrested for assault and battery.

- You are not required to answer any man's questions regarding whether or not you are wearing panties. There are no laws that require you to wear panties.

- If the man you are dating is not smart enough to complete his own homework or exams, then you should find a smarter man and you may want to report his academic misconduct to the university that he attends.

OUTRAGEOUS DATING EXPERIENCE # 12

Oh No He Didn't Tell Me He Was A Pharmacist, But He Was Really An Intern!

One spring evening I was walking from the bowling alley in Atlantic Station heading to my car and I met a gentleman. We struck up a conversation and he told me that he was a pharmacist, he was divorced, he was in his thirties, he had two children, and he would like to get to know me better. We exchanged telephone numbers and he said that he would give me a call later that evening. ("Mr. Prescription").

Mr. Prescription called me later that evening and we continued our getting to know one another conversation. Mr. Prescription told me about his ex-wife, how he let her keep their former marital home, how she had bad financial management skills, and that she was about to lose their former marital home to foreclosure. Mr. Prescription told me where he was currently working as a pharmacist and he told me all about his elaborate plans to open his own pharmacy. During every telephone conversation with Mr. Prescription he had something negative to say about his ex-wife and he told me about his plans to open his own pharmacy.

Despite Mr. Prescription's repeated ex-wife bashing and pharmacy bragging telephone conversations, I agreed to go on a date with him because I thought that maybe the in-person conversation would be better than the telephone conversations. So, I decided that we should go to the movies for our first date so that we would have time for some conversation and then I could enjoy at least part of the date even if I didn't enjoy his conversation.

After we made our date plans I went on Georgia's Secretary of State License Verification website to verify that he was a pharmacist. To my surprise I discovered that Mr. Prescription wasn't a pharmacist, he was actually a pharmacist intern. Oh No He Didn't! repeatedly tell me he was a pharmacist when he was only an intern.

According to Georgia law, Official Code Section 26-4-46, the following individuals shall be eligible to be licensed as a pharmacy intern: (1) a student that is currently enrolled in a approved school or college of pharmacy; or (2) a person who has graduated from an approved school or college of pharmacy who is currently licensed by the board for the purpose of obtaining practical experience as a requirement for licensure as a pharmacist. Pharmacy interns are authorized to engage in the practice of pharmacy under the supervision of a pharmacist and a pharmacist may be assisted by and directly supervise one pharmacy intern. In summary, an intern is not a pharmacist and a pharmacy intern can't open a pharmacy!

After I discovered that Mr. Prescription was a pharmacy intern and not a pharmacist I decided that I wasn't going to mention it to him immediately. I wanted to see how long he was going to keep pretending that he was a pharmacist. As planned, I met Mr. Prescription at the movies for our date. Mr. Prescription made some additional statements about all of his plans for opening his own pharmacy while we were waiting for the movie to start. This was the first time I was thrilled that the movie previews actually started and I didn't mind that there were a million of them. Thankfully, the movie started immediately after the previews. I don't even remember which movie we watched, but it was better than listening to him talk.

After the movie ended Mr. Prescription asked me if I wanted to get something to eat at a nearby restaurant. I agreed to go to the restaurant with Mr. Prescription for a quick bite to eat. The restaurant was within walking distance across the parking lot, so we decided to walk to it. As we were walking across the parking lot, Mr. Prescription wanted me to see what kind of car he had so he decided that he would tap the button on his hand held remote so his car horn would sound. Oh No He Didn't!

I didn't even give him the satisfaction he wanted! When his car horn sounded I didn't even turn my head to see which direction the sound was coming from. I just kept on walking with my head facing towards the restaurant. All of his grandstanding was too much for me. I knew in my mind that it was almost time to let him know that I wasn't impressed with him and that I knew he wasn't a pharmacist.

After we got to the restaurant I did my best to pretend that I was enjoying my meal and his conversation. However, I seriously felt tortured. I so wanted to tell him that he was a total fake, but I decided that I would spare him a bit of embarrassment and do it on the telephone rather than in person. I managed to make it until the end of our date without letting the cat out of the bag.

Mr. Prescription called me after our movie date. He started another bragging session about his pharmacy. I finally had to ask him how he was going to open a pharmacy when according to the Secretary of State he was only a pharmacy intern. Mr. Prescription was speechless. Then Mr. Prescription told me that he was waiting for his test results to come back and that is why he was still listed as an intern (where have I heard that one before…Outrageous Dating Experience # 9). I didn't know whether or not he was really waiting for his test results because I couldn't find out when the pharmacy exam results were released; however, I told Mr. Prescription that he was lying. Mr. Prescription was put on Don't Answer Status that night! I haven't spoken to him or heard from him since!

Advice for Men:

- If you are trying to impress a woman by bragging, then brag about the facts. Don't brag about things that you want to be true but aren't.

- For the divorced men: If and when you go on a first date with a woman, don't mention your ex-wife more than three times. Literally start keeping track of how many times you mention your ex-wife to others. Once you actually start counting how many times you mention your ex-wife to others, then you may realize that this is really not attractive to a woman during a date or a conversation.

- Don't repeatedly discuss the issues you had/have with your ex-wife. You should be discussing current events, issues that you may be dealing with at work, organizations that you are involved with, issues going on in her life, or celebrity gossip.

Advice for Women:

- If the man you are dating is repeatedly discussing how gracious he was in the divorce and he gave his ex-wife

OH NO HE DIDN'T!

everything she wanted, etc…and you really want to find out how contentious the divorce proceedings were, then get a copy of the Divorce lawsuit proceedings docket from the county where it was filed.

- o The more items that are listed on the docket (i.e. the more pleadings, motions, hearings, Court Orders, etc. that were filed in the case), the bigger the battle was between them.

- o Suppose you wanted to find the website to verify a divorce filing for a man living in Houston, Texas. You would start by going on your favorite internet search website and typing in the following (similar) search terms: Harris County Texas Divorce Docket. The website for the Harris County District Court Clerk's web page will appear in the search results. Then click on the web page. Next, click the link for Online Services and then click the link for the Search Our Records and Documents page. Then you will type in the name you are searching for, hit enter and then any cases that have been filed would appear.

- If you want additional information regarding your bragging man's divorce, then get a copy of the Divorce Agreement between him and his ex-wife. This is also a public record document available from the county where the divorce was filed.

- If a man is repeatedly telling you that he graciously gave his former marital residence to his ex-wife and you want to verify this information, then check for a Quit Claim Deed filing in the county public records where the property is located.

- Public records documents are always available in person at the County's courthouse. Some public records documents are also available on the county's website.

OUTRAGEOUS DATING EXPERIENCE # 13

Oh No He Didn't Tell Me He Wanted Me To Call Him Daddy!

In October 2009 I decided to go out for a rare Friday night of partying in Atlanta. After deciding to go, out it was time to get dressed for the evening. I put on my new INC International Concepts black slacks with my new INC International Concepts white long tuxedo shirt and my bronze Gucci peep-toe pumps and matching Gucci mini handbag. Then I drove to the High Museum of Art to meet up with my girlfriend so that we could check out the Friday night live jazz event. However, when I got there I could not tell if I really wanted to stay there so I decided that we should meet at Phipps Mall and select one of the restaurants for our night of partying. So we ended up at Twist Restaurant and Tapas Bar.

We found a spot at the bar to join in with the crowd. There was a small group of men that we began socializing with. I began talking with one of the men in the group for an extended period of time. After about 30 minutes of talking to him, two less than attractive Amazon women walked over and just moved me out of the way. When these women came over and moved me out of the way I found it extremely funny because I am not generally moved out of the way by anyone. While these women were talking to my new male friend I just started talking with other men that were in the bar area. I also had a brief conversation with a man in the bar area that had been repeatedly trying to get my attention.

The Amazon women were there for about 10 minutes and then wandered back to their table in the dining area. My male friend told me that the women had been talking with them before we had arrived and they had been seated over at a table. He said the Amazon women had returned to the bar area to invite him to sit with them; they told him that they would buy him dinner and drinks if he would come sit with them. I told him to feel free to go with them to their dinner table.

I told my girlfriend that I found these Amazon women totally hilarious because they were offering to buy this man dinner and drinks and they still couldn't get him to pay them any attention, yet he was buying me whatever I wanted as I continued socializing with him.

After he declined their dinner and drink invitation we continued our conversation. Then he wanted me to take his telephone number to call him. I told him that I was not taking his telephone number to call him, but I would be more than happy to give him my number so that he could call me. He did not want to accept the fact that I was not going to take his telephone number and call him first. ("Mr. Domineering").

Mr. Domineering got a major attitude about this and then finally decided that he would take my telephone number. Immediately after Mr. Domineering got my telephone number he stood in the middle of the noisy bar area and called me. Mr. Domineering left me a voice mail message that he was following my instructions and calling me first. Shortly after Mr. Domineering left the voice message I decided it was time to leave the restaurant.

I spoke with Mr. Domineering after I got home from the restaurant. He told me that he was single, in his thirties, never married, two children (by two different women), and he worked in sales and real estate. I asked Mr. Domineering why he hadn't married either of his baby mommas and he got offended. Mr. Domineering said that the use of the term "baby momma" was so negative and derogatory and he didn't understand why people had to refer to the mother of his children in that manner. Well we were even because I didn't understand why a grown man that already had one child with a woman that he never married decided to have another child with another woman that he wasn't interested in marrying. During that same telephone conversation he mumbled something about calling him daddy; however, I had no clue what he was talking about so I totally ignored it.

Mr. Domineering and I had a few conversations on Saturday and discussed going out to a party that evening. However, I was too exhausted from the work that I had done during the day getting my law firm client files organized. We spoke on the phone again and Mr. Domineering referred to me as momma and mumbled something about daddy. Again, I was totally clueless and disregarded his mumbling.

On Sunday Mr. Domineering called me while I was on the telephone talking to one of my girlfriend's so I let his call go to voicemail. Mr. Domineering didn't like the fact that I didn't answer his call, so he decided that he needed to call me over and over again (at least three times) until I personally answered his call. I told Mr. Domineering that I was on another call and I would call him back when I got off the phone with my girlfriend. Then, I called Mr. Domineering back and he didn't answer my call. Oh No He Didn't! Of course he wasn't calling about an emergency or even anything important. Mr. Domineering just didn't want me to continue my conversation with someone other than him while he was trying to speak with me.

The next day I was heading to the south side of town to change the address on my driver's license so I called my girlfriend and planned to meet her for lunch at my favorite pizzeria on that side of town. As luck would have it the driver's license office was closed, so I just ended up meeting my girlfriend for lunch a bit earlier than we originally planned. As I was waiting for her to arrive at the restaurant I decided to give Mr. Domineering a call. Mr. Domineering asked me what I was doing and I told him that I was at the restaurant waiting for my girlfriend to arrive.

Mr. Domineering then asked me who my girlfriend was. I told Mr. Domineering who she was and that we had gone to law school together. Mr. Domineering then said who told you that you could go to lunch with her? I told Mr. Domineering that there were several people that told me that I could go to lunch with her: I told myself that I could go to lunch with her, my friend told me that I could go to lunch with her, and her mom told her that she could go to lunch with me because her mom agreed to babysit her kids when they arrived home from school. Mr. Domineering told me that I hadn't gotten permission from Daddy to go to lunch with her. Oh No He Didn't! Who in the hell was Daddy? I know he didn't think that I was going to call him Daddy? I know he didn't think that he was my Daddy? I had one father and he died when I was 10 years old. Hell, I didn't even call my father daddy, I called him Dad.

Then he had the nerve to tell me that he wanted me to call him Daddy. Oh No He Didn't! I told him that I would not be calling him daddy. Then as he was trying to debate this foolishness with me my girlfriend arrived at the restaurant and I told him that I was getting off the telephone because she had just arrived. Mr. Domineering had the nerve to tell me that I didn't have permission to get off the phone with him yet. Oh No He Didn't! I told Mr. Domineering that I gave myself permission to get off the phone with him and that I was hanging up the phone. I then hung up the phone and turned it off. Mr. Domineering had the nerve to call back after I had turned the telephone off and left me a voice message stating that I was rude for hanging up on him. Oh No He Didn't!

I promptly deleted his message and then gave myself permission to change his name in my address book to Don't Answer Status! That was the last communication I had with Daddy!

Advice for Men:

- Don't tell a woman that you barely know that you want her to call you "Daddy." Don't call a woman that you barely know "Momma."
- If you call a woman and she doesn't answer your call, it is perfectly acceptable to leave her a voice mail message

for her to return your call. It is ignorant to call her repeatedly in an effort to get her to personally answer your call because you don't want to wait for her to call you back when she has time to speak with you.

- If you feel the need to be on control of the social calendar and the social communications of a woman that you just met, then you have some major control issues that should be immediately addressed with a professional counselor.

Advice for Women:

- Make sure you give significant thought to the consequences of having unprotected sex with and/or having a child with someone that already has multiple children with multiple women BEFORE you decide to have unprotected sex with him. Having a child changes your life FOREVER, which is more than a million times longer than the time it took to create the child!
- If a man asks you to call him Daddy, then understand that he is trying to control and dominate your life.

- If a man tells you that you need his permission to socialize with your friends, then you need to find another man to date.
- If you continue dating and end up marrying a man like Mr. Domineering, then keep in mind that you may not live to get a divorce from his controlling behavior.

Mrs. Dorene Seidl was in the process of moving out of her marital residence, she returned to the home to get a few things and her husband, William, shot and killed her.http://www.courier-journal.com/article/20100319/NEWS01/3190362/Man-convicted-of-killing-wife.

OUTRAGEOUS DATING EXPERIENCE # 14

Oh No He Didn't Ask Me What Was Wrong With Me Because He Needed To Know Up Front Before He Got Too Involved With Me!

As I said in the prior Chapters, I really enjoy the NFL football season. In January 2010 I went out several weekends to watch the NFL playoff games at local sports bars. On Saturday night, January 9, 2010, I decided that I was going out to watch the playoff game between the Philadelphia Eagles and the Dallas Cowboys, at Stats Sports Bar and Restaurant in downtown Atlanta. I went out to watch the game by myself because I actually prefer going to sports bars alone because by the end of the game I am never watching the game by myself. I have repeatedly told my single female friends that the best time to meet single men is during the NFL playoff season and during the NBA playoff season, the men are all out watching the games and there are plenty of games on television to go out and watch. I have also told my single female friends that the best pickup line is "who are you rooting for." It is simple and works every time. Another wonderful way for women to meet men during the playoff seasons is to wear a shirt for one of the teams that is playing in the game. It works really well for me because I enjoy NFL football and NBA basketball so I have no problems when a man wants to strike up a conversation about the team that I am supporting via my outfit. I am not sure how well the "team outfit" approach will work for the non-sports enthusiast, but I am sure that it is worth giving it a try.

For the Eagles versus the Cowboys game I wanted the Dallas Cowboys to win so I was wearing a blue and white outfit. I arrived at Stats and I had to stand for a little while to scope out the bar area. I ordered myself a glass of diet coke (I had a shot of Belvedere after I parked my car and before I walked into the bar, so a diet coke was the best option at that point) and started watching the game. Then, a gentleman motioned for me to join him at the seat next to him at the bar. He was attractive, so I decided to take him up on his offer and joined him at the bar. He offered to buy me a drink so I ordered an apple martini with Belvedere; however, they were out of Belvedere. That meant an apple martini was out of the question for me. I ended up getting a glass of wine instead.

We then started the general get to know you conversation: name, where do you work, what do you do for a living, are you single, do you have kids, etc. Because I told him that I was single, hadn't been married and no kids he said well what's wrong with you because I need to know up front before I get too involved with you. Oh No He Didn't! ("Mr. Tactful").

I should have immediately left Mr. Tactful's ass at the bar after he said this to me. However, I just told Mr. Tactful that there was nothing wrong with me and I did my best to continue with the conversation. We continued our conversation at the bar for a while as we watched the game. Then, we joined a group of his friends at a table in the restaurant area. Mr. Tactful ordered food for us and then left me with his friends while he went back to the bar area to continue socializing with some other females he had met.

How tacky! However, since I had just met him I didn't say anything about it. I just enjoyed the conversation at the table with the group and watched the football game.

Mr. Tactful returned to the dinner table long after his food had arrived. I ate a piece of carrot cake while waiting for him to return to his fried buffalo wings and French fries. When he rejoined us at the table we continued watching the football game. Then, I thought we were both leaving when the Dallas cowboys had secured their victory. However, I thought wrong. Mr. Tactful walked me to the parking garage and paid for my parking (I think that was to make sure that I was leaving). He walked me to my car and then claimed that he had to go back to the restaurant because the bartender hadn't closed out his tab and he had to get his credit card. Whatever! Mr. Tactful didn't owe me any explanations and I really didn't care what he did for the rest of the evening.

My mission for the evening had been accomplished: I went out, watched the football game, my team won, I met a man that took my mind off the other man that I was dating, I had a few drinks, and I had an overall nice evening. Let's keep it real...Mr. Tactful knew that he was on his way back into the bar to continue socializing with the other women that he was talking to throughout the evening.

On Sunday afternoon I went out to a different sports bar to watch the next round of afternoon NFL playoff games. I went to Fox Sports Grill in Atlantic Station and sat alone at a table for four in the bar area. This was the only table available in the bar area and it turned out to be a great table for socializing. A handsome man that was in a large group standing at the table next to mine asked me if he could use one of the chairs at my table. I smiled and jokingly told him no. Shortly thereafter we started talking because he thought that I was at the table waiting for others to join me. He ended up joining me at my table to watch the game and for an extended discussion about the NFL playoff games, the teams I predicted would be in the Super bowl (my predictions were 100% accurate this year), and whether or not Bret Farve should have stayed retired this year.

After there was no way on earth that the New England Patriots were going to recover from the massive beat down that the Baltimore Ravens put on them, we wrapped up our discussion, we exchanged telephone numbers, and then he treated me to lunch. I left Fox Sports

Grill to watch the second NFL playoff game of the day at home. Later in the evening (and after the second game was over) I ended up meeting him for drinks before he caught his flight home to Texas.

Anyway, back to Mr. Tactful. I managed to send a few text messages back and forth with Mr. Tactful while I was watching the game at Fox Sports Grill. Ironically, Mr. Tactful ended up at Fox Sports Grill at the same time I was there; however, because the restaurant and bar area was very spacious and their heating system wasn't working (in other words it was freezing in the restaurant) Mr. Tactful didn't stay long so he didn't even notice that I was at the restaurant. Additionally, I never told him that I was there. I didn't owe him any explanation regarding my Sunday afternoon whereabouts, just as he didn't owe me any explanations about going back into the sports bar on Saturday night to continue socializing with the other women that he was socializing with while he was also socializing with me.

We spoke on the telephone about the upcoming week and made plans for our first date. Mr. Tactful told me that he had tickets to the Atlanta Hawks versus the Phoenix Suns game on Friday and asked me if I wanted to go to the game with him. I told Mr. Tactful that I would love to go to the game since I hadn't been to a Hawks game since the 2009 Atlanta Hawks versus the Boston Celtics playoff series.

On Monday we exchanged a few text messages during the day while he was in a training course and while I was at work. I also sent my girlfriend an email letting her know that I had met a guy that was originally from the same area where she currently lives; she told me to find out what high school he went to because her husband grew up in the area and maybe he knew him. So right before I left work I sent Mr. Tactful a text message asking him what high school he went to because one of my best friends husband grew up in the same city he was originally from and maybe they knew each other. By the time I got outside to my car in the parking garage Mr. Tactful sent me a text message asking me if I was trying to do a background check on him because I asked him what high school he attended. Oh No He Didn't!

I sent Mr. Tactful a text message telling him that if asking what high school he went to was too personal a question for him, then I really didn't need to be involved with him. Mr. Tactful replied that he was just joking and then told me what high school and college he attended.

Later that evening we had a chance to talk on the telephone. I was doing my best to deal with his repeated less than tactful statements and text messages. However, every time we spoke or exchanged text messages it grew more and more difficult.

On Wednesday evening I called Mr. Tactful when I was on the way home from the mall and he told me that he was studying for class. So I said well go ahead and finish studying and I will give you a call when I get home from the mall. Mr. Tactful said okay but you sure are bossy. Oh No He Didn't! Here I am thinking I am being caring, considerate, and helpful in saying go ahead and take care of your homework first and then talk to me after you have taken care of your number one priority and he tells me that I am being bossy. Honestly, my life would have been fine if I had never spoken to Mr. Tactful again. However, I refrained from cussing Mr. Tactful out and actually spoke with Mr. Tactful later in the evening after I got home from the mall.

On Thursday we again exchanged text messages while he was in class and I was at work. After Mr. Tactful got out of class for the evening he gave me a call. Mr. Tactful filled me in on what he had accomplished in class that day. Then Mr. Tactful decided it was time to have another discussion about what was wrong with me because I was single, never married, and childless. I again told Mr. Tactful that there was nothing wrong with me, not everyone gets married at the same time in life, and not everyone has children at the same time in life. I told Mr. Tactful that I had been engaged previously and it didn't work out. Next, I told Mr. Tactful that I had several men offering their sperm to father a child with me in 2006; however, I wasn't up for having a child with just any man that was offering me his sperm. Lastly, I told Mr. Tactful that I would get married and have kids on God's schedule, not on his or any other man's schedule.

Then, I asked Mr. Tactful what was wrong with him because he was divorced. You know he didn't have an answer for that question. Then, Mr. Tactful apologized for his comments and I told him there was no need to apologize and there was no need for us to have this discussion again. Mr. Tactful then said that he would be on his best behavior for our Friday night date because he was really looking forward to it.

Friday finally arrived and by the grace of God we were still on speaking terms. After Mr. Tactful got out of class he called me so that we could discuss meeting for our date. We decided to meet at Philips Arena immediately before the Atlanta Hawks versus the Phoenix Suns game started. I drove to the State Bar of Georgia parking garage and then as I was walking over to the arena I met up with Mr. Tactful. Mr. Tactful gave me a hug and then we held hands and walked the rest of the way to Phillips arena.

Once we got into the arena we stopped at the concession stand. Mr. Tactful asked if I wanted anything to eat and I told him no because I had already eaten at home (I am a picky eater so I decided that eating a Lean Cuisine pizza at home before heading out for the game was the best food option for the both of us). I told him that I would get something to drink after he got his food. Mr. Tactful got a sandwich and a beverage and then we headed to our seats for the start of the game. Mr. Tactful handed me the tickets for our seats so that I could give them to the usher to guide us in the proper direction. Or, maybe he handed me the tickets so that I could see that he had purchased excellent tickets that were over $120 each. We had lower level center court seats.

OH NO HE DIDN'T!

I entered the row first and ended up sitting next to a lady that was a bit too large for her seat, so she was partially in my seat as well. Mr. Tactful sat in the seat on the left side of me and the seat next to him was empty. We got settled into our seats and then Mr. Tactful started eating his sandwich and discovered that I didn't have anything to drink. Mr. Tactful asked me if I wanted something to drink. I told Mr. Tactful that I wanted some white wine later and that I wanted him to enjoy eating his sandwich. I told Mr. Tactful at least three times that he should go ahead and enjoy his sandwich and I would be fine without a beverage until halftime. However, Mr. Tactful refused to listen to me and jumped up to run and get me some wine before the game started. While I appreciated Mr. Tactful's efforts to get me a drink, I would have appreciated it more if he had listened to my request to wait to get something to drink until after he had finished his meal so that I could've gone with him to check out the beverage selections and I could've ordered something that I would have enjoyed. The wine that he brought me was horrible, but I drank as much of it as I could because he went to the trouble to go get it for me.

ATTORNEY LISA D. WRIGHT

As we were watching the game I was leaning over towards my left and into Mr. Tactful's personal space because the lady sitting on my right was spilling over into my seat. I explained to Mr. Tactful the reason that I was sitting so close to him was because I didn't have a lot of room on my right side and I hoped he didn't mind my sitting so close to him. Mr. Tactful told me that we could switch seats. I told him that I wasn't interested in switching seats with him and that I was only explaining the situation to him to share a private moment with him during our date.

Then, Mr. Tactful told me that we could just move over by one seat because the seats next to us were empty. I told Mr. Tactful that I was not moving seats either. About five minutes after Mr. Tactful mentioned moving to the empty seat next to him, two ladies arrived to sit next to him.

As we continued watching the game the lady sitting next to me was literally using my hip as her armrest. Then, she was using my lap as her coat rack. She was actually providing me with tons of comic relief during the date. I told Mr. Tactful about her use of my hip and my lap for her personal gain and Mr. Tactful told me that we would definitely switch seats at halftime. I told Mr. Tactful that the seating arrangement was not a problem for me and I didn't want to switch seats with him because that would be rude and I didn't want to hurt the lady's feelings. She wasn't doing anything on purpose or to be rude, it was just a matter of circumstance. I repeatedly told him that I was only sharing the situation with him to share some private funny moments with him during our date. I wasn't sharing it with him for him to take corrective action. However, Mr. Tactful refused to listen to me and kept saying that we were going to switch seats.

During the second quarter Mr. Tactful decided to strike up a conversation with the two ladies that were sitting next to him (and that he had just met). The longer Mr. Tactful continued talking with these two ladies, the angrier I got and the more intensely I tried to focus my attention on the game. Then, Mr. Tactful had the nerve to ask me if I wanted to share some of their snacks and candy with him. Oh No He Didn't! He was lucky that I didn't stand up in my seat, in the middle of the game, and yell out at the top of my lungs that I wasn't interested in sharing any snacks or candy with anyone. I just quietly and politely declined the offer and continued watching the game.

Halftime finally arrived. We left our seats and went to get some more refreshments. Mr. Tactful got a warm pretzel and a beer and then he asked me if I wanted anything. I told Mr. Tactful that I just wanted something sweet. The first concession stand we went to listed chocolate chip cookies on the menu; however, they didn't have any chocolate chip cookies (typical Atlanta). The next concession area we passed was selling ice cream and Mr. Tactful asked me if I wanted ice cream. I told Mr. Tactful that I don't eat ice cream and we continued walking to see what the other concession stands had for dessert. However, Mr. Tactful appeared to have an attitude that we were walking around looking for what I wanted.

After walking for about five minutes, Mr. Tactful said I don't understand why you couldn't just get the ice cream. I told Mr. Tactful that I don't eat ice cream and I didn't want ice cream, so that was why I couldn't just get the ice cream. I also told Mr. Tactful that I didn't have to get anything and I could just go back to the seat and get ready to watch the second half of the game. Mr. Tactful and I continued walking around checking out the menus of the other concession stands; however, there weren't really any other dessert options.

As we were walking back to the entrance for our seats, we passed the ice cream concession stand again and Mr. Tactful said I just don't understand why you can't just get the ice cream. Oh No He Didn't! At that point I didn't understand why he couldn't comprehend English. I turned around and headed for the nearest exit and walked right on out of Philips Arena. I never looked back and as I was walking to my car I put Mr. Tactful on Don't Answer Status.

I didn't have to worry about arguing with him about switching seats, or being rude to the lady sitting next to me, about him continuing his conversation with the ladies next to us, or about his sharing snacks with the ladies next to us, or being asked about why I didn't want to get ice cream. I watched the end of the basketball game on television from the comforts of my own home! The Atlanta Hawks won the game!

Advice for Men:

- Don't ask a woman that you just met and that you are interested in getting to know better what is wrong with her because she is single and doesn't have children.
- If you are out at a party or a bar and it is a social meeting place, it is okay to socialize with more than one woman that is there. However, conduct yourself in a respectable manner. Don't ask a woman to sit with your friends and then leave her to go socialize with other women in the bar/restaurant while she's still sitting with your friends.
- If you are on a first date with a woman, then do not socialize with other women that you just met.

Advice for Women:

- If you are feeling disrespected and/or frustrated by a man's conversation, then you have every right to set the record straight, to change the subject, or to abruptly end the conversation with him.
- If you are feeling embarrassed and/or humiliated by a man because he is more interested in talking and flirting

with the other women around you, then don't feel obligated to continue in the situation.

- If you are having a horrendous first date and it has become unbearable, then you have every right to leave immediately. You are not obligated to remain on the date simply because he has paid for the date. You are not a prostitute and he did not purchase you for the evening.

OUTRAGEOUS DATING EXPERIENCE # 15

Oh No He Didn't Tell Me It Was Hard Going Through A Divorce When No Divorce Had Ever Been Filed!

As discussed in Outrageous Dating Experience # 6, On Sunday, November 8, 2009, I went to the Atlanta Falcons versus the Washington Redskins NFL Football game. At halftime my girlfriend and I went down to the lower level to socialize and I ran into a male friend of mine that also went to Duke University's Fuqua School of Business. He was actually one of the first classmates that I met when I initially started the MBA program in the Fall of 1996 (after completing the MBA orientation program I was accepted into the Law School from the waiting list, so I deferred my admission into the MBA program until Fall 1997 and started at the Law School in Fall 1996).

As I was standing there talking with my Fuqua classmate, I could sense that there was a man staring at me in the distance. I glanced over at him a few times and said to myself I know him from somewhere. Then my mind clicked and I asked my classmate if he was at the game with the man because the man staring at me also went to Fuqua but he graduated before us. Before my classmate could answer my question I waived the man over to where we were standing and confirmed that he was also a Fuqua graduate. (Mr. Alumni). Then the three of us started discussing our post Fuqua MBA careers, and Mr. Alumni said that he had left corporate America and he was a self-employed owner of two franchises in the Atlanta area. As the three of us were talking, his cousin and his cousin's best friend were talking to my girlfriend about the Falcons and the Redskins. Before halftime ended Mr. Alumni and I exchanged cell phone numbers. Then my girlfriend and I headed back to our seats.

After my girlfriend and I got back to our seats we had a discussion about Mr. Alumni. I told her that I had seen him several times while I was in school at Fuqua because he returned regularly to campus to host his former employer's corporate recruiting events; he was married the last time that I saw him at a recruiting event and I remembered him discussing his wife and showing pictures of his kids. At the game he didn't have a wedding band on and there were no tans lines or anything to suggest that he had been wearing a wedding band recently. I told my girlfriend I would have to ask Mr. Alumni what happened with him and his wife. Shortly after we finished our conversation about Mr. Alumni, the Falcons scored a touchdown and this was a perfect opportunity to send Mr. Alumni a text message. I sent him a simple, yet effective, text message: Go Falcons! Mr. Alumni liked my text message and responded to my text by asking me what I was doing after the game and if I wanted to go out for drinks. Mission accomplished!

Of course I told Mr. Alumni I didn't have anything planned after the game and I would love to go out after the game. However, I actually had been working on setting up plans to meet up with the man from Outrageous Dating Experience # 6, but since I knew Mr. Alumni from Fuqua and he was cuter than #6, I opted for the date with Mr. Alumni. By the middle of the fourth quarter the Falcons were leading the game and my girlfriend and I decided it was time for us to start heading out of the Georgia Dome. As we were walking into the concourse area we saw Mr. Alumni, his cousin, and his cousin's best friend. Mr. Alumni offered to give me a ride to my place to pick up my car; however, I politely declined because I preferred to walk home from the Georgia Dome to avoid any potential traffic delays so that I could get home to handle some urgent personal matters before heading to the restaurant for our date. I ended up leaving my girlfriend behind to chat with Mr. Alumni and his crew.

It took me about twenty minutes to walk home from the Georgia Dome. I changed out of my Falcons shirt and into my blue and silver Express v-neck shirt, then headed to Dantanna's Surf, Turf & Turf Buckhead Upscale Sports Restaurant for our date. While I was on the way to meet Mr. Alumni I called him to ask if he was already at the restaurant waiting for me because I wanted to make a quick stop across the street at Lennox Mall to buy a Godiva dark chocolate candy bar (that is my favorite candy bar). Mr. Alumni said he was already at the restaurant, but he didn't mind if I stopped at Godiva first. Thankfully, when I got to Lennox there was a parking space in the front row next to the entrance closest to the Godiva store so that I could dash quickly into the mall. However, when I got to Godiva there was someone in line taking what seemed like forever. I finally got my dark chocolate candy bar and then headed across the street to the restaurant to meet Mr. Alumni.

Mr. Alumni was sitting at an outdoor table at the restaurant waiting for me to arrive. The restaurant was very nice, except for all of the smoke in the air from the other patrons that were smoking. We had a flat screen television at our table so we had the waiter change the station so that we could watch the Detroit Lions versus the Seattle Scahawks game at our table. I am from Detroit, so I am a quiet Lions fan because the Lions are not one of the best teams in the NFL, but us Detroiters have to stick together and cheer for them anyway. Once the television was properly setup, Mr. Alumni ordered a beer and I ordered a diet coke.

As we watched the football game we talked about everything. I asked him about his wife (and kids) that I recalled him discussing when I saw him at Fuqua campus recruiting events. Mr. Alumni said that he had been married for ten years, his wife was ten years older than him, she was focused on her career, they had grown apart, they were no longer interested in the same things, he had nothing negative to say about her, and it was hard because he was going through a divorce. Mr. Alumni said that his wife was content with the life they were living and she wanted nothing more out of life; however, he wanted more out of life than he had currently achieved. Then we started discussing our respective careers since graduating from Duke.

It started getting too cool to sit outside so we moved to an inside table. Then we ordered some food. The Lions were trying to win; however, they couldn't pull off a victory. About three hours after we started our date and shortly after the football game ended we decided it was time for our date to end. Mr. Alumni walked me to my car, gave me a hug and told me that he wanted to see me again. After we left the restaurant we exchanged a few more text messages. After I got home from our date, I went online and checked the online public court records for the county that I thought Mr. Alumni resided in to verify that a divorce was pending. However, there was no divorce pending that included his name. Then I checked in the other surrounding counties and

I didn't find his name listed anywhere. Oh No He Didn't!
tell me it was hard going through a divorce when no divorce
was pending!

The only excuse that I have for continuing to
communicate with Mr. Alumni after finding out this
information was that I gave him too much benefit of the
doubt because of an "Alumni Connection," meaning when I
encountered him previously he was honest and straight
forward. I decided that I would ask him about his statements
and about the information I gathered (Note: I wasn't
planning on specifically telling him that I had looked at the
public records and his name wasn't listed, I had to be subtle
with the information at this point).

The next day we exchanged text messages throughout
the course of the day while I was at work. After I got off
work he called me and we discussed when we would see
each other again. Mr. Alumni asked me when he could come
over to see me and my city view. I told Mr. Alumni that he
could buy me dinner and visit me on Tuesday because I was
too tired for socializing that evening.

On Tuesday we exchanged text messages throughout
the day. I got off work at 4pm and Mr. Alumni was at my

place before 5pm. I allowed Mr. Alumni to come up to my place to check out my downtown view before he took me to get dinner. I told him that there were several restaurant choices in my building for us to choose from. Mr. Alumni told me to select the one that I wanted, so I chose the Mexican restaurant. We went to the Mexican restaurant and had dinner, then returned back to my place to watch a basketball game.

As we were watching television Mr. Alumni noticed that I had an iPod nano and asked me if he gave me the money would I go to the store and get him an iPod and then load it with music for him. Mr. Alumni said that he wanted an iPod because he was flying to the Caribbean with his kids for Thanksgiving and he wanted to use it on his flights. I told Mr. Alumni that I would be more than happy to go get it for him on Wednesday because I was planning on shopping at the Mall of Georgia area stores and I had plenty of time to shop for it and to load the music and videos on it for him because I would be off from work for Veteran's Day. Then we went on the internet to figure out which iPod he should get: the nano, the touch 8GB, or the touch 32GB. We decided that the iPod touch 8GB would be the best option for him. He took out $200 from his wallet, told me he was a butt man, and then put the money into my back jean pocket. We said our good bye for the evening and then I walked him down to the parking garage.

On Wednesday, I went to the Staples store across the street from the Mall of Georgia and purchased the iPod touch 8GB for Mr. Alumni using a Staples store credit that I had from a prior return. I also made sure that I put the purchase on my Staples rewards card to get the points for the $210 purchase. Therefore, my name and contact information was on the receipt for Mr. Alumni's iPod touch. I used the $200 cash that Mr. Alumni gave me to purchase shoes and clothes from some other stores that afternoon.

I sent Mr. Alumni a text that I got his iPod for him and that I was on the way home to load it with music and videos. I completed my shopping at the Mall of Georgia and then headed home to work on Mr. Alumni's iPod. After about 2 hours, Mr. Alumni and I had matching iPod's. I had successfully loaded his iPod with everything that was loaded on my iPod. I absolutely loved his iPod touch. I was almost ready to tell Mr Alumni that I wanted him to buy me an iPod touch too!

Mr. Alumni came over Wednesday night to see me and his new iPod touch. I told Mr. Alumni that he should definitely get a carrying case and that I would be more than happy to pick one up for him. Mr. Alumni asked me to please get him the carrying case and gave me the money for it. Mr. Alumni then asked me if the $200 had been enough for the iPod touch and I told him that there was $10 in sales tax, so he gave me the additional $10. Mr. Alumni visited with me for about four hours that night.

Mr. Alumni came over again on Thursday evening after I got off work. This was the evening I decided to ask him about the status of his divorce. Mr. Alumni told me that he and his wife were just trying to work out all of the financial details before they actually filed for the divorce. As a lawyer this sounded logical because I had handled several divorce cases where the husband and wife had already agreed upon the terms of the divorce and I just had to draft up the written divorce agreement to file with the Petition for Divorce, and when both documents were filed simultaneously the divorce was granted in thirty days.

I told Mr. Alumni that I didn't want to end up on CHEATERS® (the television show that uses surveillance cameras to show viewers actual true stories, filmed live, documenting the pain of a spouse or lover caused by infidelity) or SNAPPED® (a television program on Oprah's Oxygen Network that profiles women that have been charged with murder ...and the reasons they have snapped..including finding out that they have a cheating husband). Mr. Alumni looked at me like I was crazy for even suggesting that we would be on either show. Mr. Alumni then told me to be patient, just give him some time to get everything taken care of.

On Saturday while I was out running errands I went to Best Buy to get a protective carrying case for Mr. Alumni's iPod touch. I found the last one in the store that was on sale. When I bought it I made sure that I gave the cashier my Best Buy Rewards Zone account number to include the purchase on my rewards account. The receipt for the purchase included my name and my Best Buy Rewards Zone account number.

The following Monday, Mr. Alumni sent me a text message that his dad was in town and he wanted me to meet him. I told Mr. Alumni that I would love to meet his dad. Mr. Alumni said that he would pick me up around 8pm so that he could take us both out to dinner. Mr. Alumni called when he was on his way to pick me up. I was waiting for Mr. Alumni in the lobby of my building when he arrived with his dad. His dad opened the car door for me and allowed me to sit in the front seat. Mr. Alumni reached over and gave me a kiss and then we were on our way to dinner at Houston's Restaurant on Peachtree Street in Atlanta. We had a nice time at dinner. Mr. Alumni was the perfect date. His dad started grilling me about why I didn't have children and asking me if I wanted to have children. Mr. Alumni could tell that the conversation was getting difficult for me and he told his dad that I would be a great mother and took over the conversation for me. After dinner Mr. Alumni drove me home and walked me to my door, he gave me a long hug good-bye and then left to drive his dad home.

Mr. Alumni came over to visit me on Tuesday evening while his dad was out on a date. He told me that his dad enjoyed our dinner and looked forward to us socializing together in the future. Socializing with Mr. Alumni and his dad gave Mr. Alumni's divorce claims some additional credibility. After we finished discussing the fun we had during Monday night's dinner, then I let him watch a basketball game instead of making him watch my absolute favorite Tuesday night television show, The Biggest Loser. Mr. Alumni was special, so he got special treatment. That evening I told Mr. Alumni that I had mentioned him to my coworkers but I was wondering if I should not have because he was married and it would not be that difficult for them to figure out who he was. I asked Mr. Alumni if I was a secret. Mr. Alumni told me no, we are not a secret! We enjoyed the rest of our evening and when Mr. Alumni left for the evening he took his iPod touch, protective carrying case, and the receipts with him.

On Thursday afternoon Mr. Alumni sent me a text message that he had spent three hours shopping for my birthday gift. I was so excited and looking forward to finding out what Mr. Alumni got me. That evening Mr. Alumni came over to visit. I asked Mr. Alumni if he was coming over on Sunday for my birthday and he said he didn't know but he would make sure that I got my birthday gifts. Oh No He Didn't!

After he left, I sent him a text message that if he couldn't make time for me on my birthday, then he could keep the gifts and then I turned my phone off for the night.

The next morning when I woke up for work and turned my phone on there was a text message from Mr. Alumni that he was just joking about not coming over for my birthday. My bad! We both apologized for the misunderstanding and then sent several text messages throughout the day.

It was finally Sunday, my 40th birthday and time to get my gifts from Mr. Alumni. Mr. Alumni arrived at 11am with lots of gifts! He got me scratch off lottery tickets (we both loved those things), a gift basket full of Godiva chocolates and a Godiva gift card (he remembered that I stopped at Godiva on the way to our first date), and a gift certificate for a half day of spa services at Spa Sydell! Mr. Alumni made my birthday totally worth celebrating, he was so incredibly special! After I opened my gifts we just sat and talked for a couple of hours. Then I took myself to the mall and to the movies.

Mr. Alumni came over on Monday and Tuesday evening before he left on his international trip for Thanksgiving. Mr. Alumni claimed that his wife wasn't going on the trip with him and that only he and the kids were going. However, I didn't believe him and I didn't really care because I had just met him two weeks before, so if he had planned a family trip for Thanksgiving before I met him then I didn't have a problem with it. I just told Mr. Alumni to make sure that he brought me a gift back. Mr. Alumni was gone for a week that seemed like forever. However, we sent text messages back and forth daily to each other.

When Mr. Alumni returned from his holiday vacation, he sent me a text that he was back in town. I was thrilled and I couldn't wait to see him. Mr. Alumni came over and gave me a hug that let me know just how much he cared for me and missed me while he was gone. Mr. Alumni didn't bring me a gift from his vacation because he claimed that his child left the bag of gifts on the hotel shuttle bus. However, he knew exactly what to do and how to make me happy, he brought me a "substitute" gift. Mr. Alumni brought me a big bottle of Belvedere Vodka because he knew that it was my favorite.

The next week, on Tuesday December 8, 2009, when I got back in town from my business trip, Mr. Alumni came over to visit me and told me that one of his best friends was having a party on Saturday. Mr. Alumni asked me if I wanted to go to the party with him. I told Mr. Alumni that I would love to go to the party with him and that I would like to meet his friend because he had mentioned him on several occasions. The next day I flew out of town for another overnight business trip.

I flew back into Atlanta on Thursday evening and went to the Macy's at Lennox mall to shop for an outfit to wear to the party. I ended up missing the holiday party at my condo because I was at Macy's longer than I had planned. I didn't end up buying anything; however, I ended up with some specific outfits in mind that I could purchase before the party on Saturday night. When I got home from the mall I sent Mr. Alumni a text message about my visit to the mall and told him about the outfits I had in mind for the party. Mr. Alumni told me that he couldn't take me to the party as his date because his friend's wife called his wife and invited her and the kids to the party....so he had to take his wife and kids to the party. Oh No He Didn't! just un-invite me to the party!

On Friday Mr. Alumni and I discussed whether or not he was going to come over to visit me. Initially we decided that he was going to come over around 10pm and then he told me that he was also planning to take me to breakfast on Saturday morning. I figured that since he was planning to take me to breakfast and it was cold out that he could just wait and take me to breakfast in the morning and I would stay in and work on getting my holiday cards addressed and ready to mail. I sent Mr. Alumni a text message that he didn't have to come over because it was cold out and he could just take me out to breakfast in the morning. Mr. Alumni didn't like that text message. Mr. Alumni wrongly assumed that I was planning on going out with someone else for the evening and that's why I told him not to come over.

If I were planning to go out with someone else for the evening, then I would not have invited him to come over in the first place. Additionally, he was planning on spending the evening at home with his wife so what right did he have to get mad about my Friday evening plans. Anyway, I had no clue that Mr. Alumni was mad. I spent my Friday evening working on my Christmas cards and talking to my mom on the telephone.

Saturday morning I woke up and sent a text to Mr. Alumni asking him if he was still taking me to breakfast. Mr. Alumni told me no because it was still cold outside. This is when I figured out that he was mad at me for telling him that he didn't have to come over. So I told him that we needed to talk in person because we needed to clear the air. He told me that we could meet for lunch. We decided to meet for lunch at Houston's Restaurant near Lennox because I was going to be in that area Christmas shopping and he was going to be in that area working.

I was highly pissed off when I got to the restaurant (I was already un-invited to the damn party and then he was clowning about my boring ass Friday night home alone) so I knew that I needed a glass of wine as soon as I sat down because I didn't want to wind up saying the wrong thing during our lunch. I actually ended up drinking the glass of wine that he already had for himself at the table when I arrived. He had to order another glass of wine for himself. We both calmed down, had a nice lunch, and everything was back to normal by the end of our lunch. I told him to go to the party with his family and make the best of it, even if I had been uninvited. Mr. Alumni told me that he didn't even want to go to the party because I wasn't going with him. He always knew what to say.

After we left the restaurant I went to Lennox mall and got his Christmas gift from the Louis Vuitton store. While we were at lunch I told him he would have to act right for 14 days because the Louis Vuitton store had a 14 day return policy and that was where I was getting his gift from and if he didn't act right I would be returning his gift. Saturday night while Mr. Alumni was at the party with his wife and kids he sent me text messages all night long. He told me about the people that were at the party and the music. I kept telling Mr. Alumni to stop texting me with the details of the party because I didn't want to know about it. He just ignored me and kept sending me updates. I finally told him to just suck it up and try to have a good time and enjoy the party. Mr. Alumni promised to make amends on Sunday for uninviting me to the party, then he asked me if I would make us breakfast in the morning. I told Mr. Alumni yes and I would see him in the morning.

On Sunday morning Mr. Alumni was at my place by 9am. I made us breakfast in bed. Then we had a wonderful morning in bed before getting ready to go to the Georgia Dome. We both had tickets for the Atlanta Falcons versus the New Orleans Saints NFL football game. Mr. Alumni was supposed to go to the game with a friend, but there was a last minute change and he ended up calling his dad to go with him to the game. We got dressed for the game and then

I rode with him to pick up his dad. Mr. Alumni's dad actually lives in close proximity to Mr. Alumni's marital residence, but since Mr. Alumni wasn't too overly concerned about my riding in the car with him I wasn't going to let him know that I was a bit concerned about what would have happened if his wife had seen me riding in the Escalade with him. But we managed to make it to his dad's place safely.

As soon as Mr. Alumni's dad got into the Escalade with us he wanted to start talking about the Saturday night party. I told his dad that I didn't want to hear anything about the party. Then his dad told me that I shouldn't be mad about not attending the party because I didn't miss much. Mr. Alumni did his best to get his dad to stop talking about the party. We finally changed the subject and then had a nice conversation for the rest of the ride to the Georgia Dome. When we got into the Georgia Dome, Mr. Alumni gave me some money to get drinks for my girlfriend and me and then he and his dad headed to their seats. We met back up with Mr. Alumni and his dad during halftime and then after the game.

Over the next week things were going really good with Mr. Alumni and me, as we continued to joke that I didn't want to have to return his Christmas gift to the Louis Vuitton store. However, Mr. Alumni was not so happy that I was planning to spend my Christmas in Detroit with my family. I kept telling him that there was no way I was going to spend my holiday here in Atlanta without any of my family around while he spent the majority of his Christmas holiday with his wife, kids, and the rest of his family. I told Mr. Alumni that we would celebrate our Christmas together after I returned from Detroit, on Tuesday, December 29, 2009.

While I was in Detroit for the Christmas holiday Mr. Alumni and I were in touch daily, we spoke and sent text messages frequently.

On Monday the 28th I headed to the Detroit airport to fly back to Atlanta. Mr. Alumni called me while I was waiting to board my flight and told me how cold it was in Atlanta. I told him that it was snowing in Detroit, so I would be okay with the cold in Atlanta. After we got off the phone we stayed in touch by exchanging text messages. Mr. Alumni sent me a text that he was out bowling with his kids. I told him I hope that he wasn't getting beat too bad. I sent Mr. Alumni a text when I got on the plane and told him that I would text him when I landed in Atlanta. My flight back to Atlanta was uneventful and I landed on time. As promised, I sent a text to Mr. Alumni when I landed. Then, I took the train home from the airport and got ready for what I thought was going to be a great Tuesday… work and then the Christmas celebration/gift exchange with Mr. Alumni.

I woke up Tuesday morning around 6:15am, turned on my cell phone and there was a text message for me that reminded me of the voice mail message that Tiger Woods left for his mistress when his wife went through his phone. Mr. Alumni sent me a text message that said: wife went thru my phone, if she calls you tell her you don't work for me anymore. Oh No He Didn't! When did I ever work for Mr. Alumni? Why in the hell was Mr. Alumni telling anyone that I worked for him? What in the hell was going on?

Deep down I knew that this was the beginning of the end, BUT I knew that I deserved my Christmas gifts and I was going to get my gifts! God gave me the strength to get ready for work that morning. Of course I forwarded Mr. Alumni's text message to a few friends. When I got to work I sent Mr. Alumni a text to find out what in the hell was going on…and to find out if we were still doing our gift exchange that evening. Of course Mr. Alumni said that he couldn't see me that evening for the gift exchange because he had to lay low for a couple of days. He told me that he would call me and give me the details of what happened.

Mr. Alumni called me about an hour later and told me that his wife had gone thru his cell phone and read the text messages that I had sent him the night before and that she had found the iPod receipts with my name on them. Mr. Alumni then said that his wife asked him who I was and his dumb ass told her that I used to work for him at one of his businesses. Mr. Alumni then told me that if Mrs. Alumni called me just tell her that I no longer worked for him. Yeah right! Mr. Alumni was really starting to act like he had absolutely lost his damn mind.

Mr. Alumni sent me a text message a few hours later asking if his wife had called me. I ignored it. Then he called me from his cell phone. I didn't answer his call so he left me a voice mail message asking me if his wife had called me. I called Mr. Alumni back and lied to him. I told Mr. Alumni that I received several calls that day, but I hadn't been able to answer them and there were some voice mail messages on my phone that I hadn't checked yet so she could have called me, but I wasn't sure. Mr. Alumni told me that his wife had been acting strange all day so he was wondering if she had called me. Mr. Alumni was sweating bullets all day long. That's what happens when you lie to your wife and to your mistress!

Our communications via text and telephone were limited over the next few days. Thankfully, I had a few other men in the pipeline to keep me busy while I waited to see Mr. Alumni and to get my Christmas gifts. On December 30th I started making plans with another gentleman for New Year's Eve, since I knew that it was highly unlikely that I would be spending it with Mr. Alumni. Of course I was correct. On New Year's Eve Mr. Alumni told me that he would take me to lunch on New Year's Day to make up for the time we hadn't seen each other. Whatever! On December 31st I had a first date with another man. It was a nice evening, even if it wasn't with Mr. Alumni.

On January 1st Mr. Alumni called me and told me he was on his way over to take me out to lunch. Mr. Alumni picked me up around 1pm and decided we were going to a Mexican restaurant on Peachtree. When I got in the

Escalade with Mr. Alumni I didn't have much to say and he did the majority of the talking. Mr. Alumni told me about how his wife let him know that she had gone through his cell phone...she didn't explicitly say that she went thru his phone she just started calling him hey babe over and over again because that is how I started off my text messages to him. Mr. Alumni said Mrs. Alumni's sister was also having marital problems and that was probably why she decided to go through his cell phone.

Mr. Alumni said he was extremely mad that she went through his cell phone and he just couldn't believe that she had read the text messages in his phone because that was an invasion of his privacy. Then he said that he anticipated her filing for divorce within two weeks and he was going to let her file for the divorce because he wanted her to feel like she was winning the battle by filing for the divorce instead of him. He also said that he didn't care about anything financial; he just wanted to be able to see his kids.

I didn't have much to say. I asked him what happened to my Christmas gifts. Mr. Alumni said that he couldn't get my Christmas gifts out of the house because his family was home, so we would have to exchange gifts the

197

following week. I just had to keep telling myself to keep hanging in there for a few more days to get my gifts.

We got to the restaurant and I remained pretty quiet. Things between us just weren't the same. I usually like Mexican food and sangria; however, I hated the food and the sangria that I ordered. Mr. Alumni asked me what I did for New Year's Eve and I told him that I had a date. Mr. Alumni got an attitude about it so I had to ask if he really expected me to sit at home and cry over him all night long. NOT! Mr. Alumni asked me if I had a nice time on my date. I told him yes, I had a nice time but it wasn't the same as spending the evening with him. Mr. Alumni said: "you are mad at me aren't you." I said: "yes." Then he said: "but the hard part is that you love me, don't you." I said: "yes, that's the hard part about all of this." We left the restaurant shortly thereafter.

As we were walking to his Escalade, Mr. Alumni decided that he wasn't going to open the door for me to get in because he was still mad that I had gone out on a New Year's Eve date with someone else. He told me that my date from the prior evening could open the door for me. So I asked him who he spent the prior evening with, he said Mrs.

Alumni...and then he came to his senses and opened the door for me to get into the Escalade. We rode back to my place and then he stayed to visit with me for a couple of hours.

Mrs. Alumni put him on lockdown in 2010! There weren't too many more weekday evening visits and when Mr. Alumni came to visit me in the evenings he only stayed for an hour or two. I told myself that I could deal with this drama until February 1st, at the latest. If Mr. Alumni wasn't moved out of his marital residence by February 1st, then I would be moving on with my life without him.

On Monday January 4th it was finally the day for our Christmas gift exchange. Mr. Alumni came over after I got off work. I gave him a Louis Vuitton Petit Damier Cap and a Starbucks gift card. Mr. Alumni gave me a Gucci gift card and a Target Stores gift card. I was thrilled! He wouldn't tell me the amounts on either gift card, so I left out at the same time I was walking him to his Escalade. Mr. Alumni asked me where I was going and I told him I was heading for the Gucci store to find out the value of my gift card and to start shopping. My babe got me the perfect gifts, even though I was delayed in getting them by a week. I was very pleased when I found out the value of both gift cards. Mr. Alumni was very happy with his gifts as well.

Mr. Alumni was supposed to come watch the NFL Playoff games with me on January 9th. But at the last minute he claimed that he was not feeling well from the pizza he ate. I am not stupid; I knew that Mrs. Alumni had him on lockdown so he couldn't come over. That's why I went out for the evening to watch the game and I told him that I was going out to watch the game.

On January 15th during my lunch break, I went to the Gucci store at Phipps to get a pair of Gucci shoes that were on sale with the Christmas gift card from Mr. Alumni. The shoes were fabulous and the price was unbelievable. As I was leaving the Gucci store I sent a text message to Mr. Alumni thanking him for my Gucci gift card and letting him know that I got a pair of shoes. I also sent him a picture of the shoes that I purchased with the gift card. About ten minutes after I left the mall, as I was driving back to work, I received a call that came up as Unknown (I had been receiving a series of calls that kept displaying the number as Unknown ever since Mrs. Alumni went through his cell phone, but I hadn't been answering the calls and whoever was calling never left a message).

I finally decided today was the day that I was ready to talk to Mrs. Alumni because I was tired of her calling me (my intuition knows that she was the person calling me over and over again) and if she wanted to know what was going on, then I was finally ready to tell her. I answered the call and said hello. I caught the woman on the other end (i.e. Mrs. Alumni) totally off guard when I answered the call. She said ah, hey girl, did he call you back yet? (She was trying to pretend that she was one of my friends calling, but my friends know me and know that I may have more than one man in my life at a time so they would not call me and ask if "he" called me back, they would ask me about him by his name). I responded to her by asking her well who is he. Then she said ah, ah, ah, I have the wrong number. I really wanted to say no, Mrs. Alumni you don't have the wrong number, what is it that you would really like to say to me or what is it that you would like to know. But I didn't and the call ended. When I got off the phone I was wondering if she was either reading his text messages on the internet or if she had gotten a second cell phone and she was receiving copies of his text messages simultaneously. I never told Mr. Alumni about that call. Life with Mr. Alumni was getting too complicated for me, and I have always preferred to keep things simple. This was why I didn't date married men! On Saturday January 16th I sent Mr. Alumni a text message asking him if the divorce had been filed yet. (I already knew that nothing had been filed because I had checked in the public records). Mr. Alumni responded that he thought I was letting him handle things. I told Mr. Alumni that every married man tells his mistress that he is handling things. Then I told Mr. Alumni that my definition of him handling things would include him providing me (1) details of when he would be meeting with a divorce attorney (2) providing me details of when he would be moving out of his marital residence, and (3) providing me with details of where he would be moving to: either to an apartment of his own, to his father's place, or moving in with me. I expected Mr. Alumni to ignore this text message because he had ignored my prior requests for similar information in the past. However, this time he actually responded by asking if I really meant it when I said that he could move in with me. I sent Mr. Alumni a text message reply that I was serious and he could move in with me if he needed to. Of course I knew Mr. Alumni's text message could have meant one of two things: either he was just trying to appease me and tell me that he was thinking of moving in with me or he was really working on his divorce plans.

Sunday night Mr. Alumni sent me a text message asking me if we could meet for breakfast. Of course he said he missed me. I told Mr. Alumni that I missed him too and we could meet for breakfast. I asked Mr. Alumni where he wanted to meet. He replied he wanted breakfast at my place. I totally got suckered into agreeing to that one. Anyway, by 10am the next morning Mr. Alumni was at my place for a Martin Luther King, Jr. Holiday breakfast in bed celebration. I didn't want to get into a heated discussion by asking him for additional details about when he was actually planning to move in with me. So we just enjoyed each other's company and just chilled out for a few hours. Mr. Alumni actually fell asleep for about an hour and he was snoring so loudly that I was actually considering remaining on mistress status and allowing Mrs. Alumni to keep him for nights and weekends. However, when Mr. Alumni woke up he apologized for his snoring and I told him I would let him stay with me despite his loud ass snoring.

On Thursday, January 21st around 9pm my cell phone rang and this time a telephone number that I didn't recognize was displayed, but I felt like it had something to do with the telephone call that I received the prior Friday because earlier in the day I had received two telephone calls from an Unknown number. I decided that I would answer the call because I was tired of these telephone calls and I was ready to get the conversation with Mrs. Alumni done and over with.

When I answered the call there was a female voice, but she had an African accent and it was a different voice than the woman that called me the prior Friday. This woman yelled to me to stop calling her boyfriend. I wanted to interrupt her and say didn't she mean her husband, but I decided that I would just let her continue. I asked her who are you and who is your boyfriend. She told me that I knew who her boyfriend was and I told her that I didn't know who her boyfriend was because she hadn't told me who he was. Then she told me that she knew I liked to send lots of text messages to him.

I told her that it was true that I liked to send lots of text messages and that I regularly send lots of text messages to men, but I wasn't sure who her man was so I couldn't confirm if I liked to send text messages to her man or not. Then she told me that she thought she knew who I was and I better watch my back. I again asked her who she was and who her man was. She refused to answer my questions. Lastly, she told me if I wanted to know who her man was then I should send another text to her man and then she would call me right back and I would know who she was and I would know who her man was.

Well, that sounded like a challenge to me...and I love to take on a challenge. So, I called my girlfriend in Texas to tell her about the conversation and she gave me the best idea. After I got off the telephone with my girlfriend I sent Mr. Alumni a text message that said some lady called me tonight and told me to stop calling you and texting you, so do you think that means she wants me to stop ******* you too? I figured that if she was reading his text messages, then she would enjoy that one the best. I am not sure if she read it or not, but she never called me back.

ATTORNEY LISA D. WRIGHT

The next morning I got a text message from Mr. Alumni thanking me for letting him know about the call I received. This really didn't sound like a message from Mr. Alumni and it really made me wonder if Mrs. Alumni was reading and now responding to his text messages over the internet. But Mr. Alumni called me a couple of hours later and confirmed that he was the one that sent me the text message. I told him about all of the details of the telephone call and he said he didn't know anything about it. I said to Mr. Alumni that I knew it had something to do with Mrs. Alumni, even if I couldn't prove it, it was either one of her friends or one of her employees that called. Lastly, I told Mr. Alumni that I wasn't lying to anyone about anything, whether it was by telephone or by text.

On Saturday morning Mr. Alumni came over to visit me. Mr. Alumni told me that he and the men at the barbershop where he gets his hair cut discussed the fact that Mrs. Alumni had gone through his cell phone and the mystery telephone call that I received. He said that the men were laughing at him and that they were shocked that he didn't have a separate cell phone line for calling and texting with me. I told him that if I got any more strange calls, then he was definitely getting a second telephone line so that we could text and talk freely.

I again asked Mr. Alumni how long he had been married and he said almost eleven years. I asked him couldn't he hang in there another eleven years and then that would make it twenty-two years; he told me no, he couldn't take another eleven years. He told me that I just didn't understand. I told him it was his decision and a major decision, especially because he had children. Mr. Alumni told me he had made up his mind and he was getting a divorce.

Then we moved onto discussing our future living arrangements. I told Mr. Alumni that my lease expired in July so if he wanted us to live somewhere else, then he needed to let me know sooner rather than later. Mr. Alumni asked me if I wanted to continue living downtown or if I wanted us to live in a house. I told Mr. Alumni I wanted us to live wherever he wanted us to live. Then I asked Mr. Alumni when he was planning on moving in with me and he said the summer. Oh No He Didn't! just tell me with a straight face that he was going to keep living with his wife for the second half of the winter, all of the spring, and then he was going to move in with me in the summer!

I didn't say a word, I just smiled and said to myself I don't think that I am going to even make it until my February 1st deadline to dump him. It was time for Mr. Alumni to get back to his franchise, so I walked him to his Escalade and then I headed out to run errands. I stopped at my cell phone provider's store to get a replacement Blackberry. Despite Mr. Alumni's "moving in with me in the summer" comment, while I was at the store I checked into adding a second line on my plan and I checked out the prices for the various cell phones in case Mr. Alumni needed to get a second phone to communicate with me. I sent Mr. Alumni a text message with the pricing information but we both decided that it wasn't the right time to get the second line.

As I predicted, I didn't make it to the February 1st deadline. On Sunday, January 24th I got another call from an Unknown number. This was the straw that broke the camel's back. I was so done with Mr. Alumni, Mrs. Alumni, calls from unknown numbers, and calls from strange women. I called Mr. Alumni and told him it was over, I was tired of the drama, and I was tired of all of the lies he had been telling since November. Of course he wanted to play dumb on the lies…so I said to him you told me that you were going thru a divorce on our first date but no divorce had ever been filed, then you told me that you were working on settling the financial issues with Mrs. Alumni so that the two of you could file for the divorce, and then when Mrs. Alumni found out that you were having an affair with me you told me that you didn't give a damn about money all you wanted was to be able to see your kids. After I read him the riot act, then Mr. Alumni had the nerve to ask me if Mrs. Alumni calls would I just not say anything about the two of us for the sake of his family. Oh No He Didn't! just ask me to lie for him when he had been lying to me for the last three months!

Since January 24th, I have not heard from Mr. or Mrs. Alumni. I have not had any additional calls from any unknown callers and I have not had any additional calls from any women that refuse to identify themselves. Lastly, as of March 30, 2010, neither Mr. Alumni nor Mrs. Alumni has filed for divorce.

Advice for Men:

- If you are married, then the only woman that you should be dating is your wife.

- If you are married and you want to date and have sex with women other than your wife, then get a divorce first.

- If you decide to that you are going to ignore my first and second points of advice and date someone other than your wife, then don't lie to the woman that you are dating and tell her that you have filed for divorce when you haven't. (You will have more than enough opportunities to lie to your wife during this time, so you don't need the extra burden of lying to your mistress as well.) Tell your potential girlfriend that you have no plans to divorce your wife and let her decide whether or not she wants to continue a relationship with you.

- If you have no plans to leave your wife and you don't want your wife to find out that you have a girlfriend, then make sure you keep all of the information regarding your girlfriend away from your wife. Don't take receipts to your marital home with your girlfriend's name, address and telephone number on them; don't leave your girlfriend's name and telephone number saved in your cell phone; and don't leave text messages to and from your girlfriend saved on your cell phone for your wife to find them.

- If you have been lying to your girlfriend about the status of the relationship with your wife, then don't ask your girlfriend to lie for you. Under these circumstances your mistress is not going to be interested in lying to your wife or to anyone else in order to protect you.

Advice for Women:

- Don't date married men. Life is much easier when you only date single men.
- If you meet a married man and he tells you that he is in the process of getting a divorce, then IMMEDIATELY check the public court records to verify that he is really a party to a divorce case.
- If a married man has lied to you and told you that he has filed for divorce and you find out that he hasn't, then

stop dating him immediately. Don't give him the benefit of the doubt!

- If you decide that you want to knowingly and willingly date a married man, then date him at your own risk. Additionally, tell him that you are not lying to anyone about anything. So he won't be surprised when you don't agree to lie to his wife about your relationship with him.

- There are no laws in favor of mistresses, so your married boyfriend doesn't owe you any apologies or money or anything else when he stops dating you to return to exclusivity with his wife.

- In Hawaii, Illinois, Mississippi, New Hampshire, New Mexico, North Carolina, South Dakota and Utah there are laws against infidelity and you could find that your married boyfriend's wife has filed a lawsuit against you for alienation of affection. His wife may end up with a judgment against you!

SUMMARY OF DATING ADVICE FOR MEN

- If you are a convicted felon, don't try to date an attorney.
- Don't try to associate yourself with a group that you are not a member of to make women think that you are a member of that group.
- If the woman you are planning to take on a date doesn't know your friend, then don't offer to have your friend pick her up for the date.
- Don't tell a woman that you will never call her again and then continue calling and texting her.
- Don't volunteer to perform tasks for a woman that you know you don't have the skills to perform.
- If you tell a woman that you have completed something for her with the assistance of someone else, then make sure that your assistant is competent to assist you in getting the job done AND that the job was done BEFORE you tell the woman that you have completed the task for her.

- If you don't have the money to pay for a date an hour before the date, then don't confirm the date an hour before the date.

- When you don't have the money to pay for a specific type of date, then don't try to take a woman on that type of date.

- Take your date on the type of date that you can afford, but don't make it look like you are a cheapskate.

- Don't send text messages with pornographic pictures to women that are not interested in dating you.

- Don't let your male ego put you in a position of having to defend yourself in a criminal proceeding for harassing a woman that you barely even know because your feelings are hurt that she is not interested in dating you.

- If a woman specifically tells you that she is not interested in getting to know you, then believe her and move on to meeting the next woman.

- Don't tell a woman that you are celibate and then tell her that you love to have oral sex as often as you can.

- Not every woman wants to get married and have kids with every man she meets, so if you just want to have a sexual relationship with a woman, then just tell her that up front. If she doesn't want the same type of relationship, then you can both move on quickly.

- Don't try to use your physical strength to force a woman do what you want her to do.

- Treat women exactly how you want them to treat you… because payback is a bitch!

- If you stand a woman up for a date, then don't expect to get another date with her.

- Do not lie on your online dating profile by putting an entire photo album of photographs of you wearing clothes that you can no longer fit. In other words, if you have gained weight and can't wear any of the clothes that you are wearing in the pictures, then don't put any of those pictures on your dating profile.

- When a woman tells you that she would rather go home and watch television than have a second beverage with you, she is politely telling you that she is not interested in continuing the date.

- If a woman politely tells you that she is not interested in dating you, then accept it graciously and move onto meeting the next woman.

- If you have children (no matter how old they are), then check the box that says yes for the question regarding do you have children on the online dating profile questionnaire.

- List the ages of your children in your profile so that someone viewing your profile will have the information they need to decide if they want to date you with the children that you have.

- If you actually plan on meeting the women that you are communicating with from internet dating websites, then don't lie on your profile about your height by more than one inch.

- Don't lie about your profession, especially when it is a licensed profession that can be easily verified.

- If a woman that you have only dated once catches you in a major lie, then just give up on dating her. Don't keep telling more lies in an effort to try and continue dating her.

- When a woman is trying to keep the getting to know you conversation going, don't insult her by telling her it seems like she likes to talk a lot.

- When you are celebrating New Year's Eve with your date, don't tell her that you are counting how many glasses of champagne she is having and how much food she is eating.

- Don't tell the woman you are dating that she is a knucklehead. In the event that you feel that she is a knucklehead and you want to tell someone that you feel this way, then tell it to everyone else in the world but her!

- When you don't like your date's outfit you have several options, none of which should include telling her that she is naked.

  o Option 1: You can choose to say nothing about her outfit, continue with the date and then never see her again.

  o Option 2: You can choose to say nothing about her outfit but offer her your coat or jacket for her to wear so that it will cover up her outfit.

- o Option 3: You can find a favorable way to discuss her outfit, such as complimenting her on the color of her outfit or her shoes or anything that you can find that you like about her outfit. Once the two of you start discussing her outfit, then you can find out if she either loves her outfit and always dresses in this manner or if she hates her outfit and would not dress in this manner in the future. Keep in mind that one day you are probably going to wear an outfit that she hates and she isn't going to tell you that you look like a hot mess!
- If are dating a woman and you are not in a sexually intimate relationship with her, then DO NOT ask her if she is wearing panties. No matter how bad you want to know the answer to that question, do not ask her! That is not an appropriate date question.
- Don't ask a woman that you are dating to do your school homework or exams for you because you could find yourself expelled from school for academic misconduct if she reports your unethical behavior to the school.

- If you are trying to impress a woman by bragging, then brag about the facts. Don't brag about things that you want to be true but aren't.

- For the divorced men: If and when you go on a first date with a woman, don't mention your ex-wife more than three times. Literally start keeping track of how many times you mention your ex-wife to others. Once you actually start counting how many times you mention your ex-wife to others, then you may realize that this is really not attractive to a woman during a date or a conversation.

- Don't repeatedly discuss the issues you had/have with your ex-wife. You should be discussing current events, issues that you may be dealing with at work, organizations that you are involved with, issues going on in her life, or celebrity gossip.

- Don't tell a woman that you barely know that you want her to call you "Daddy." Don't call a woman that you barely know "Momma."

- If you call a woman and she doesn't answer your call, it is perfectly acceptable to leave her a voice mail message for her to return your call. It is ignorant to call her repeatedly in an effort to get her to personally answer your call because you don't want to wait for her to call you back when she has time to speak with you.

- If you feel the need to be on control of the social calendar and the social communications of a woman you just met, then you have some major control issues that should be immediately addressed with a professional counselor.

- Don't ask a woman that you just met and that you are interested in getting to know better what is wrong with her because she is single and doesn't have children.

- If you are out at a party or a bar and it is a social meeting place, it is okay to socialize with more than one woman that is there. However, conduct yourself in a respectable manner. Don't ask a woman to sit with your friends and then leave her to go socialize with other women in the bar/restaurant while she's still sitting with your friends.

- If you are on a first date with a woman, then do not socialize with other women that you just met.

- If you are married, then the only woman that you should be dating is your wife.

- If you are married and you want to date and have sex with women other than your wife, then get a divorce first.

- If you decide to that you are going to ignore my first and second points of advice and date someone other than your wife, then don't lie to the woman that you are dating and tell her that you have filed for divorce when you haven't. (You will have more than enough opportunities to lie to your wife during this time, so you don't need the extra burden of lying to your mistress as well.) Tell your potential girlfriend that you have no plans to divorce your wife and let her decide whether or not she wants to continue a relationship with you.

- If you have no plans to leave your wife and you don't want your wife to find out that you have a girlfriend, then make sure you keep all of the information regarding your girlfriend away from your wife. Don't take receipts to your marital home with your girlfriend's name, address and telephone number on them; don't leave your girlfriend's name and telephone number saved in your cell phone; and don't leave text messages to and from your girlfriend saved on your cell phone for your wife to find them.

- If you have been lying to your girlfriend about the status of the relationship with your wife, then don't ask your girlfriend to lie for you. Under these circumstances your mistress is not going to be interested in lying to your wife or to anyone else in order to protect you.

SUMMARY OF DATING ADVICE FOR WOMEN

- Don't accept a Facebook friend request until you have confirmed the identity of the person making the friend request.
- Don't be afraid to reject a Facebook friend request from someone you don't know.
- Use your official State and county online criminal search internet websites to verify that the man you are about to meet is not a convicted criminal.
  - o These websites generally provide the information for free and can be found with a simple web search, for example: Georgia judiciary criminal search.
  - o The websites that appear with a .gov or a .us ending are the websites that are generally operated by the State or County offices that you will want to search.
- If you know that you are not interested in getting to know a man any further, then put him on Don't Answer Status as soon as possible.

- If you delay putting a man on Don't Answer Status because you think that the things he does that irritate you won't bother you over time, then you are kidding yourself as long as you continue dating him.
- Your time is valuable. If a man doesn't respect your time for a first date, then don't go out with him because he will never learn to respect your time in the future.
- Once you have put a man on Don't Answer Status, leave him on Don't Answer Status, even if he sends you texts daily.
- If you are not interested in dating a man with children, then don't be afraid to tell him that you are not interested in dating a man that already has children. In the event that you are reluctant to say this to him directly, then you have two options: you can send it to him via text message or you can show him a copy of this advice. I am sure that he will get the message. If he doesn't get the message when you show him this page of the book, then tell him to send me an email at attorney@lisadwright.com and I will tell him for you.
- If you have asked a man nicely to stop communicating with you and he then starts harassing you, then make

sure you save all text messages, photos, emails, etc. from him so that you will have the documentation to report it to the police.

- If you are getting harassed by a man, then don't be afraid to report him to local law enforcement. Don't try to take matters into your own hands.

- If you receive harassing or threatening communications from a man, make sure that you tell at least one family member or friend about it so that if something happens, you will have a witness to your situation if it becomes necessary in the future.

- When you are on a first date or during your first telephone conversation with a man and all he wants to talk about is sex/sex topics, then know that the only "relationship" that he wants to have with you is a sexual one.

- Know what type of relationship you want from the man before you have sex with him, you generally don't get to change it up once you have your game plan in place.

- Don't engage in detailed sexual communications with any man by text messaging.

- If you are feeling physically threatened or intimidated by a man early on in your relationship, don't continue dating him because it is only going to get worse.
- If a man stands you up for a date, you have every right to stand him up for a date.
- If you are on a date and having a horrible time, then it is okay for you to leave the date when you can no longer tolerate his ass!
- When planning a first date with a man that you have met online, make sure that you plan an activity for a short time period so that if the date isn't going great then you don't have to be there too long. If the date is going good, then you have the option to stay longer.
- Make sure that a family member or a friend knows exactly when and where you are planning to meet for your internet date. Send that person a status update or two during your date so that they know you are safe.
- Also, provide your family member or friend with the man's cell phone number so that if you were to come up missing then they would quickly know where to start searching for you.

- Make sure you have a set of internet dating "rules" that you follow such as: how many emails you want to exchange with a man before giving him your cell phone number; how long you want to communicate with a man before you have a first date; what lies from his profile are you willing to accept/what lies are deal breakers; and a list of your favorite public places where you are willing to go for your first date.

- If a man has lies on his online dating profile, don't be afraid to ask him about it. If you don't like his response, don't be afraid to move on to the next man!

- When a man tells you that he is a lawyer, doctor, or any other profession that requires a license by the State, go on the internet and verify that he is in fact licensed before you go on your first date with him.

- If you can't verify that the man is the licensed professional that he told you he is, then don't be afraid to ask him about the fact that you can't verify his license. If he is lying about his occupation, then he is also lying about other issues.

- When a man tells you that he works with or went to school with your friend (or acquaintance), then make sure you check with your friend to verify that he is telling you the truth. You can never be too careful.

- The legal definition of a "Reasonable Man" is "[A] person whose notions and standards of behavior and responsibility correspond with those generally obtained among ordinary people in our society at the present time..." R.F.V. Heuston, *Salmond On The Law of Torts* 56 (17th ed. 1977).

  o It is okay to stop dating a nice man when he totally lacks a reasonable man standard level of dating skills.

  o A man that calls you up and tells you that you are a knucklehead lacks a reasonable man standard level of dating skills!

- The relationship that a man has with his mother when you start dating him won't change based on the length of time that you date him. It is what it is, no matter how much you may want it to change it won't! Accept it as it is, or find someone else to date.

- Don't slap your date if he tells you that you're naked because your outfit is too skimpy. You don't want to get arrested for assault and battery.

- You are not required to answer any man's questions regarding whether or not you are wearing panties. There are no laws that require you to wear panties.

- If the man you are dating is not smart enough to complete his own homework or exams, then you should find a smarter man and you may want to report his academic misconduct to the university that he attends.

- If the man you are dating is repeatedly discussing how gracious he was in the divorce and he gave his ex-wife everything she wanted, etc…and you really want to find out how contentious the divorce proceedings were, then get a copy of the Divorce lawsuit proceedings docket from the county where it was filed.

  o The more items that are listed on the docket (i.e. the more pleadings, motions, hearings, Court Orders, etc. that were filed in the case), the bigger the battle was between them.

  o Suppose you wanted to find the website to verify a divorce filing for a man living in Houston, Texas. You would start by going on your favorite internet search website and typing in the following (similar) search terms: Harris County

Texas Divorce Docket. The website for the Harris County District Court Clerk's web page will appear in the search results. Then click on the web page. Next, click the link for Online Services and then click the link for the Search Our Records and Documents page. Then you will type in the name you are searching for, hit enter and then any cases that have been filed would appear.

- If you want additional information regarding your bragging man's divorce, then get a copy of the Divorce Agreement between him and his ex-wife. This is also a public record document available from the county where the divorce was filed.

- If a man is repeatedly telling you that he graciously gave his former marital residence to his ex-wife and you want to verify this information, then check for a Quit Claim Deed filing in the county public records where the property is located.

- Public records documents are always available in person at the County's courthouse. Some public records documents are also available on the county's website.

- Make sure you give significant thought to the consequences of having unprotected sex with and/or having a child with someone that already has multiple children with multiple women BEFORE you decide to have unprotected sex with him. Having a child changes your life FOREVER, which is more than a million times longer than the time it took to create the child!

- If a man asks you to call him Daddy, then understand that he is trying to control and dominate your life.

- If a man tells you that you need his permission to socialize with your friends, then you need to find another man to date.

- If you continue dating and end up marrying a man like Mr. Domineering, then keep in mind that you may not live to get a divorce from his controlling behavior. Mrs. Dorene Seidl was in the process of moving out of her marital residence, she returned to the home to get a few things and her husband, William, shot and killed her.http://www.courier-journal.com/article/20100319/NEWS01/3190362/Man-convicted of killing wife.

- If you are feeling disrespected and/or frustrated by a man's conversation, then you have every right to set the record straight, to change the subject, or to abruptly end the conversation with him.

- If you are feeling embarrassed and/or humiliated by a man because he is more interested in talking and flirting with the other women around you, then don't feel obligated to continue in the situation.

- If you are having a horrendous first date and it has become unbearable, then you have every right to leave immediately. You are not obligated to remain on the date simply because he has paid for the date. You are not a prostitute and he did not purchase you for the evening.

- Don't date married men. Life is much easier when you only date single men.

- If you meet a married man and he tells you that he is in the process of getting a divorce, then IMMEDIATELY check the public court records to verify that he is really a party to a divorce case.

- If a married man has lied to you and told you that he has filed for divorce and you find out that he hasn't, then stop dating him immediately. Don't give him the benefit of the doubt!

- If you decide that you want to knowingly and willingly date a married man, then date him at your own risk. Additionally, tell him that you are not lying to anyone about anything. So he won't be surprised when you don't agree to lie to his wife about your relationship with him.

- There are no laws in favor of mistresses, so your married boyfriend doesn't owe you any apologies or money or anything else when he stops dating you to return to exclusivity with his wife.

- In Hawaii, Illinois, Mississippi, New Hampshire, New Mexico, North Carolina, South Dakota and Utah there are laws against infidelity and you could find that your married boyfriend's wife has filed a lawsuit against you for alienation of affection. His wife may end up with a judgment against you!

DATING ADVICE - LEGAL TERMS MEN & WOMEN SHOULD KNOW!

Adultery*
Voluntary sexual intercourse between a married person and someone other than the person's spouse.

Alienation of Affections*
A tort claim for willful or malicious interference with a marriage by a third party without justification or excuse; (1) some wrongful conduct by the third party with the plaintiff's spouse, (2) the loss of affection of the plaintiff's spouse, and (3) a causal relationship between the third party's conduct and the loss of affection.

Assault*
The threat or use of force on another that causes that person to have a reasonable apprehension of imminent harmful or offensive contact; the act of putting another person in reasonable fear or apprehension of an immediate battery by means of an act amounting to an attempt or threat to commit a battery.

Battery*
The use of force against another, resulting in harmful or offensive contact.

Divorce*
The legal dissolution of a marriage by a court.

Docket*

A formal record in which a judge or court clerk briefly notes all the proceedings and filings in a court case. A judicial record.

Evidence**

Testimony, writings, or material objects offered in proof of an alleged fact or proposition. All the means by which any alleged matter of fact, the truth of which is submitted to investigation, is established or disproved. That which demonstrates, makes clear, or ascertains the truth of the very fact or point in issue, either on the one side or on the other. Direct evidence – such as the testimony of an eyewitness.

Harassment*

Words, conduct, or action that being directed at a specific person, annoys, alarms, or causes substantial emotional distress in that person and serves no legitimate purpose.

Public Record*

A record that a governmental unit is required by law to keep, such as lawsuit filings or land deeds, kept at a county courthouse. Public records are generally open to view by the public.

Restraining Order*

A court order restricting a person from harassing, threatening, and sometimes merely contacting or approaching another specified person.

Single*

An unmarried person.

Witness**

In general, one who, being present, personally sees or perceives a thing; a beholder, spectator, or eyewitness. One who testifies to what he has seen, heard, or otherwise observed. <u>Wigginton v. Order of United Commercial Travelers of America, C.C.A.Ind.</u>, 126 F.2d 659, 666.

*Black's Law Dictionary (8th Edition 2004).
** Black's Law Dictionary (6th Edition 1990).